THE SHY ASSASSIN

The soldier – that is, the great soldier – of today is not a romantic animal, dashing at forlorn hopes, animated by romantic sentiment, as to love-lady or a sovereign; but a quiet, grave man . . .

Walter Bagehot

Unhappy the land that has no heroes.

Bertold Brecht

THE SHY ASSASSIN

The inspiring story of
Cyril 'Frank' Babbage,
Battle of Britain Spitfire ace
turned D-Day Mosquito pilot

AIR MARSHAL
G.A. 'BLACK' ROBERTSON

GRUB STREET • LONDON

For the many whose contribution to the Allied victory in 1945 was neither recognised nor recorded. . .

. . . and for Nicholas. May his and subsequent generations be similarly ready to bear the burden of any future conflict.

Published by Grub Street
4 Rainham Close
London SW11 6SS

A CIP record for this title is available from the British Library

ISBN-13: 978-1-911714-26-2

Design by Myriam Bell Design UK

Printed and bound by Finidr, Czechia

CONTENTS

FOREWORD

THIS INFORMATIVE BOOK IS A fine addition to the canon of extraordinary achievements in war of largely unknown people. The known heroes, those who attracted the attention of the wartime publicity machine have mostly written their story, or had it told for them long ago, and they have taken their place in history.

The author's fascination with the story of Cyril Babbage followed a meeting with a relative, and this same family connection has been a feature of various recent books uncovering previously hidden wartime activities. One might think that plenty has been written about World War II flying exploits, but especially now when the free world is confronting a level of instability and threat not seen since the 1930s, both the media and the public could gain much from a better understanding of what a major war entails.

The book describes the desperate rush to produce pilots and aircraft to fight the war; the limited training given before being pitted against an experienced Luftwaffe; the shortage of desperately needed equipment. The Operations Record Books (ORBs), so revealing to the author and his considerable research, give vivid accounts of the losses and pressures in the Battle of Britain. One must wonder how we would survive losses today when aircraft numbers are so low and training for the range of capabilities inherent in modern combat aircraft is a matter of months rather than a few weeks.

Cyril Babbage became an ace; his survival owed much to his skills but also to luck as was the case with many of 'The Few'. He would have been an excellent instructor; his calm, low key and undemonstrative demeanour, alongside his credibility as an ace, would have been perfect for the role. It also gave him welcome 'down time' before moving to the Mosquito. I found this part of the book truly fascinating. Here again the ORBs are immensely revealing in the operations leading up to D-Day.

I would like to have known more about this remarkable man but he died quite young and whilst his logbook and numerous photos were unearthed, no personal diaries were found. I hope the reader will, like me, feel proud that our nation could muster a youth from a relatively humble background who could, without fuss, master a Spitfire, become a skilled fighter pilot, and rise through the ranks to contribute vitally to D-Day in the Mosquito, a magnificent but demanding aircraft.

To its credit, the RAF produced many young men like Babbage, heroes all, but unknown to the wider public. Black Robertson's thoughtful book shines a light on such men and can help to both educate and develop in the modern generation an understanding of the demands of war and invigorate too pride in our nation's history and its fight for freedom.

Air Chief Marshal Sir Michael Graydon GCB CBE
February 2025

INTRODUCTION

It was one of those rarities, a glorious summer's day. Hot and sunny, not a cloud in the sky, and perfect for the aerobatic displays at Duxford's Summer Air Show. Not that I saw too much of them. On 24 June 2023 I was sitting with John Davies at Grub Street's stand with a series of thrilling sights and sounds at my back, hoping to interest passing enthusiasts in a recently published book, the story of a New Zealand Spitfire pilot, Wing Commander Owen Hardy DFC*, AFC, who'd served with my father. Commissioned by his daughter, Debbie Elliott, that Saturday was the public debut of *From Spitfires to Vampires and Beyond*.

Towards the end of the afternoon, it attracted the attention of a tall, distinguished-looking individual. How long does it take and what sort of research is involved in writing such a story, he asked. It emerged that Francis Wells, a renowned consultant cardiothoracic surgeon at nearby Papworth Hospital, grew up hearing stories about the wartime career of a distant relative, a cousin once removed. He was keen to learn more about Cyril Babbage once his time-consuming medical career drew to a close. But thus far he'd found information hard to come by, hence the query.

Over the next year or so, as we became better acquainted, the possibility emerged of researching and writing Babbage's story, albeit not for some time. I had a busy schedule and another book to complete. In the interim, despite the relative paucity of information – some of it contradictory and confusing – the more I learned about Babbage's career, the more the prospect of telling his story intrigued. It was partly because a number of fascinating coincidences came to light. They acted like a magnet, drawing me in.

Here was a man who, like my father, became a Spitfire ace – albeit in more demanding circumstances, the Battle of Britain. While the trajectory of his relatively long career appeared never to have intersected with that of my father's much shorter one, their wartime experiences exhibited so many similarities that I found myself compelled to delve deeper and deeper into Babbage's background. As I did so, familiar names began to appear, characters who defined that special generation. Some, like Douglas Bader,[1] 'Johnnie' Johnson[2] and Bob Stanford Tuck,[3] were once household names; others simply provided a direct connection with my father, or even to Owen Hardy.

One of the most interesting of these links was that to Erich Rudorffer,[4] the Luftwaffe *Experte*[5] regarded as one of Germany's most accomplished fighter pilots. He shot down at least two of Babbage's colleagues. The second of them, Archie Winskill, was for a brief period my father's commanding officer (CO). His demise in North Africa came barely a month after Rudorffer effectively ended Father's own flying career. Then there was the added interest of peripheral connections with the rich and famous: David Niven, Amy Johnson and the Duke of Norfolk. It was also fascinating to find that Babbage was once invited to dinner with the father of an old acquaintance, a member of the Guinness banking family.

Tracing Babbage's career through the summer of 1940, I began to see the struggle for survival that was the Battle of Britain through a different prism, one that created a sense of familiarity. It felt at times like being a fly on the wall at a Spitfire dispersal. I came to recognise the squadron pilots, sharing in their triumphs and grieving over the occasional, inevitable loss. In short, I was all but committed – and that was before I learned of Babbage's time as a Mosquito pilot.

If his Battle of Britain experiences provided a new perspective, intimate and unusual at times but peppered throughout with characters, Babbage's Mosquito flying shed a new and very different light on the events of D-Day – its prelude and aftermath too. It brought a new understanding, not just of the magnitude of the Allies' task and extent of the necessary preparations, but also of the interactions between the main players in Operation Overlord. On the one hand, there was the enormous scale of the events of 6 June 1944 – the prior deception operation too. And on the other, the courage and daring not just of the aircrew involved, but also of the lesser-known supporting cast on the ground, those operating behind enemy lines.

If there's a common thread here, it's human frailty – the very impermanence of life. Babbage suffered the regular loss of friends and colleagues, by day in the Battle of Britain and by night over France after D-Day. Death was something he never quite got used to, no matter its regularity, no matter its inevitability.

For all that this book reveals about a man who, in his stoic acceptance of the challenges conflict brought, was typical of his generation – shy, unassuming and reserved – there is so much more that we cannot possibly know. What lay behind his occasional absences from the operations roster? How did a young man with a tendency towards introversion fit in with his more outgoing colleagues? How did he cope with the day-to-day pressures inherent in his front-line role? One possible answer is the sheer enjoyment he, like so many of his colleagues, derived simply from flying aircraft like the Spitfire and Mosquito – this plus the careless exuberance of youth. Such questions hint at the lack of evidence in some instances and gaps in the narrative elsewhere that leave the reader with a series of outlines on an otherwise blank canvas, outlines they can colour as they wish. In that sense this tribute to one of the nation's countless unsung heroes simply provides a suitable palette.

In sketching this backdrop, in the interests of authenticity primary sources are quoted verbatim, regardless of occasionally questionable syntax and unconventional typography. This is especially evident in extracts from squadron ORBs. Compiling these key historical records, a squadron commander's responsibility and classified secret at the time of writing, remains something of a chore even to this day. Completed and submitted shortly after the end of every month, it's easy to see why those tasked with preparing these important documents in times of war might have had other more important things on their minds. But for the military historian they remain a priceless gift.

Through the ORBs that frame his wartime story, and countless other sources that add substance to his achievements, it has been an education and a privilege to get to know Cyril Babbage, aka 'Cabbage' and later 'Frank' – a man who simply loved to fly. He stands surrogate for so many whose stories, sadly, we will never hear.

Black Robertson
Cheltenham, February 2025

CHAPTER 1

THE BUTCHER'S BOY

Cyril Frederick Babbage played a part in two of the most momentous events in recent British history. Airborne in his Spitfire on 15 September 1940, the day victory in the Battle of Britain is now commemorated, nearly four years later he was flying a Mosquito over occupied France in the pre-dawn darkness of D-Day, 6 June 1944. In an unlikely but not impossible parallel – certainly for a Frenchman – it's as if the same man earned his place in history by surviving the fighting at both Trafalgar in 1805 and Waterloo ten years later. And Cyril Babbage was nothing if not a survivor.

He was born on 25 June 1917 in Ludlow, Shropshire, to Beatrice (née Brookes) and Frederick Babbage. His father was from Devon, a master butcher and deputy meat agent for the area who plied his trade from a shop in the High Street, No. 14. He sold the business in 1929, but it remains there to this day. D.W. Wall & Son is one of the county's best known family butchers. Fred then moved with his family to Ross-on-Wye, and a 'rather grand' Victorian house, West Bank, on Walford Road, which now serves as a care home. While his father set up shop again at 3 Broad Street and continued in the meat business, Cyril resumed his education at Ross Grammar School.

A quiet, undemonstrative individual, like many who enjoyed successful careers as RAF aircrew, the young Babbage was an accomplished sportsman. A schoolboy cricketer and rugby player, he was also a member of the local rowing club. With the River Wye dominating the town, it was inevitable that a thriving club should develop there. Ross Rowing Club's origins go back to the 1870s and Cyril was one of a number of members who made their mark in World War II.

After leaving school, he began working in his father's business. It was very much a family affair. An uncle on his mother's side, Charles Wells, had earlier joined the enterprise in Ludlow. He lived in a grace and favour house in the grounds of Ludlow Castle but in 1926 he bought a butcher's business in the market square in Clun, a small village some 16 miles away; his family moved there the following year. Charles' wife, Gertrude, Cyril's aunt, would play a symbolic role in the young man's subsequent change of career – one driven by the looming prospect of war with Germany. It was this that prompted the young man, on 8 October 1938 at the age of 21, to sign up for the new RAF Volunteer Reserve (RAFVR) on a five-year engagement.

According to his service records, Cyril Babbage was 5 ft 6 ins tall with brown hair, blue eyes, a fresh complexion – and a scar inside his left thigh. As a 'u/t pilot', his initial training took place at Gloucester from 23 October to 6 November 1938 and included his first air experience flight in a Tiger Moth. Next came his flying training at No. 2 Flying Training School (FTS), RAF Brize Norton. Mobilised on 1 September 1939, by 17 December 742123 Sergeant C.F. Babbage had earned the right to wear the RAF flying badge, his 'wings', thus cementing his place in a fledgling organisation that would change the face of the RAF.

Had it not been for the introduction of the RAFVR in 1936, with the first volunteers signing up the following year, the service would have been in dire straits during the Battle of Britain – particularly as aircrew losses began to mount in August and September 1940. Its introduction not only helped solve a problem caused by the RAF's disorderly pre-war expansion, it contributed to a change in culture. The RAFVR was 'a true reserve for the whole Air Force; it did not have separate units of its own as the Auxiliary Air Force did. Its purpose was to teach young men with no previous service experience to fly in their spare time'.[6] No longer were recruits allocated to officer or airman cadres based on social class. Rather they entered as airmen, were allocated an aircrew category and promoted or commissioned purely on the basis of demonstrated performance. Hereinafter the RAF became more egalitarian, less a bastion of privilege – an environment where the aristocracy, the cream of society would not only rub shoulders with the common man, they would fight together side-by-side. The response to this innovation was immediate. By the outbreak of war the RAFVR strength stood at 10,217. Nearly two-thirds (6,646) of these were pilots, the remainder observers and wireless operators/air gunners.[7]

Sergeant Cyril Babbage was about to enter a different world. With no experience on type, and little in overall terms (180 hours total, just 130 solo), he found himself posted to a Spitfire squadron. It's difficult to imagine a greater challenge for an embryo fighter pilot than on-the-job training in time of war. But that's what he now faced.

CHAPTER 2

THE TWILIGHT WAR, *DRÔLE DE GUERRE*, *SITZKRIEG*

THE PERIOD OF RELATIVE INACTIVITY from September 1939 until May 1940 that became known as 'the Phoney War' was also referred to as 'the Twilight War'. In France, it became *la drôle de guerre* and in Germany, most expressively perhaps, *der Sitzkrieg*. Babbage was fortunate that his first few months on 602 Squadron fell within this period of relative quiet.

Located some 15 miles north-east of Edinburgh, close to the coast, the airfield at Drem predated the formation of the RAF.[8] In 1916 it was known as West Fenton Aerodrome. The resurfaced grass strip was renamed RAF Drem in 1939 when it played host to the various aircraft of No. 13 Service Flying Training School (SFTS): Audaxes, Harts and Oxfords. With the nation now at war, training ceased shortly after the Spitfires of No. 602 (City of Glasgow)

Squadron arrived on 13 October 1939. An Auxiliary Air Force unit within No. 13 Group, the squadron was tasked with the air defence of Edinburgh and protection of shipping in the Firth of Forth.

Luftwaffe interest in the naval bases at Scapa Flow and Rosyth led to 602 carrying out some of the earliest interceptions of the war. In fact, the squadron was the first to be credited with a Luftwaffe scalp. Three days after their arrival at Drem, Flight Lieutenant George Pinkerton and Flying Officer Archie McKellar shot down a Junkers (Ju) 88 bomber which crashed into the sea off Crail. The event prompted several congratulatory telegrams, including one from the Air Officer Commanding-in-Chief (AOC-in-C) Fighter Command, Air Chief Marshal Sir Hugh 'Stuffy' Dowding:[9] "Well done. First blood to the Auxiliaries". Many of the others, from the Chief of the Air Staff[10] (CAS) down through the RAF hierarchy, expressed a similar sentiment.

As a footnote to this achievement, it remains a contested one. There is even confusion amongst official records, some of which suggest (incorrectly) that it was a Heinkel (He) 111 rather than a Ju 88 that was shot down. It is certainly arguable that the honour of shooting down the first Luftwaffe aircraft of the war actually went to Flight Lieutenant Patrick Gifford of 603 (City of Edinburgh) Squadron, who shot down a Ju 88 off Prestonpans a matter of minutes before Pinkerton and McKellar's victim also crashed into the sea.[11]

Less than a fortnight later, on 28 October, McKellar claimed a third share in the destruction of a He 111 that crashed in the Lammermuir Hills, south of Haddington – the first aircraft to fall on British soil during World War II. As this sort of sporadic activity continued north of the border, it was enough to see the Hurricanes of 111 Squadron, under Squadron Leader Harry Broadhurst,[12] arrive from Northolt on 30 November in the hope of better pickings than had thus far been on offer 'down south'.

When the 22-year-old Cyril Babbage joined 602 Squadron on 12 December 1939, he exacerbated a growing problem: that of converting several recently arrived RAFVR aircrew to the RAF's most modern fighter. With no two-seaters for dual instruction, and the first Spitfire operational training unit (OTU) yet to form, those like him with little previous flying experience, and none on the Spitfire, faced a considerable challenge. In fact, it proved a step too far for some of the more elderly squadron members, including two who had 'outgrown their ability' to master the new aircraft and requested a transfer to the RAF's Administrative Branch.

For a neophyte, the leap in performance from trainers like the Audax and Hart to the Spitfire called for a carefully monitored squadron introduction: dual sorties in the Magister then Harvard, followed by half a dozen or so solo flights, mainly in the Magister. Just such a process led to Babbage's first Spitfire 'solo' on 27 December, followed by consolidation sorties on each of the next two days. To complete this process satisfactorily was no mean feat. The Spitfire posed considerable challenges, especially during take-off and landing. Mitchell's elegant masterpiece[13] was famously described as 'a lady in the air but a bitch on the ground'. The reasons for this latter indictment were a lengthy fuselage forward of the cockpit which pointed upwards and inhibited visibility, a narrow track undercarriage that made the aircraft somewhat skittish, and an immensely powerful engine that simply compounded the other two problems. The associated difficulties were aptly summarised by 92 Squadron's Geoffrey Wellum,[14] describing his first Spitfire sortie: "Didn't know an awful lot about that one and I feel that perhaps the aeroplane had the last laugh. She was flying me during that landing almost as much as during the take-off."[15]

Limited numbers of both Spitfires and dual-controlled trainers had earlier become a matter of concern to Babbage's flight commander, Flight Lieutenant 'Sandy' Johnstone.[16] So much so that when the squadron's Harvard first arrived, he went to considerable lengths to familiarise his new arrivals with the aircraft. A pre-war commercial pilot with over 1,000 hours to his name, Johnstone had firm ideas, one of which was to improve the standard of instrument flying on B Flight. With the prospect of plenty of night flying during the winter months, he lost no time in putting new arrivals, amongst them Sergeant Babbage and two of his non-commissioned officer (NCO) colleagues, Sergeants Bailey and McAdam, 'under the hood' with a safety pilot to monitor and encourage them. The unfortunate Bailey would soon be killed. On 30 December, aged just 19, he crashed south of the airfield when the starboard wing of his Spitfire broke off while he was practising aerobatics; he'd just completed a loop. McAdam, who began his Spitfire flying a month ahead of Babbage, would prove something of an enigma – failing to return on time from Christmas leave and eventually leaving the squadron under a cloud.

Prior to Bailey's demise, a strange incident is recorded in the squadron ORB. On 21 December, 'F/Lt. Urie F/O. Stone and F/O. McKellar opened fire on a Squadron of Hampdens. Two Hampdens were shot down.' The 602 pilots mistook the Hampdens, both of which ditched successfully with just a single fatality amongst the two four-man crews, for German Dornier (Do) 17s. The two types had a similar layout: twin engines, a narrow fuselage and twin tail fins. To add to the perpetrators' chagrin, the two remaining Hampdens landed short of fuel at Drem. Further embarrassment followed next morning when the remaining bombers took off at first light and proceeded to 'bomb' the airfield with all the toilet rolls they could muster from their overnight hosts' accommodation.

Babbage flew his first operational sortie on Tuesday 13 February 1940 – an uneventful 35 minutes. It was the first of six such 'patrols' totalling nearly six hours spread over the remainder of the month, interspersed with regular practice sorties. Four days later, after acting as target for a colleague's camera-gun attacks, he 'crashed on landing' – a bounce which collapsed the undercarriage. Fortunately, the damage was repairable and by July K9961 was flying again with 7 OTU Hawarden. His progress was interrupted on 26 February when HM King George VI visited Drem in his capacity as Air Commodore-in-Chief of the Auxiliary Air Force, a role he rather undermined by appearing in the uniform of an admiral of the fleet. He nevertheless took the opportunity to present the CO, Squadron Leader Andrew Farquhar,[17] with his recently gazetted DFC; the citation noting that he 'has led his squadron with magnificent dash and courage'.

Four days earlier, Farquhar had been involved in a bizarre incident. Together with Flying Officer George Proudman, flying the RAF's only cannon-armed Spitfire,[18] he damaged a He 111 which subsequently crash-landed at Rhodes Farm, North Berwick. Keen to avoid the crew setting fire to their aircraft before the effects of the new, albeit consistently unreliable cannon could be assessed, he landed nearby – only for his Spitfire to flip onto its back on soft ground, leaving him trapped in the cockpit. He then suffered the ignominy of being assisted from his crashed aircraft by the Heinkel crew – once they'd extricated their wounded rear gunner. Finding Farquhar trapped, the three remaining Germans used their combined strength to raise one wing far enough for the CO to release his straps and crawl out. To add insult to injury, he then found himself facing three Lugers as the crew attempted to take him prisoner. The situation was eventually resolved by the arrival of a detachment of elderly Local Defence Volunteers, forerunners of the Home Guard.

The day after the royal visit, the Air Officer Commanding (AOC) No. 13 Group, Air Vice-Marshal Richard 'Birdie' Saul,[19] who had been amongst those accompanying the King,[20] 'examined training programme and inspected logbooks. We must practise fighter attacks more.' This revealing comment in the ORB reflects the unit's relatively relaxed flying programme. Not for nothing did this period become known as the Phoney War. There was a sense of unreality amongst some 602 crews, prompted in part by the knowledge that their army and navy counterparts were engaged in a conflict that took them far from home. Aircrew, meanwhile, were able to return to their creature comforts at the end of each day: messes or, in some cases, private houses. It was an uncomfortable feeling, exacerbated by the knowledge that the AOC had rented a cottage for his wife and young daughter in Gullane, not far from Drem. With his headquarters near Newcastle, he was keen to remove his family from what he saw as a more immediate danger – circumstances that doubtless contributed to his regular visits to one of his Scottish stations.

A few examples of what the 602 Squadron ORB describes as 'Normal Routine' illustrate the challenges even experienced Spitfire pilots faced at Drem. On 1 March, 'F/O A.M. Grant crashed on Drem Aerodrome, no personal injury.' The following day, 'F/O George Victor Proudman force landed Spitfire at Dunbar, very slight apparent personal injury.' Then on 9 March, 'F/Sgt. D.W. McAdam[21] taxied L.1004 into L.1019. Slight damage to mainplane.' Found guilty by the subsequent Court of Inquiry, by the end of the month the accident-prone McAdam was posted to another unit. A regular cause of concern since his arrival in August, three incidents in late January 1940 did little for his credibility. A landing accident at Acklington left his aircraft on its back; a day later his Spitfire ended up on its nose at Drem, and the following day he attempted a wheels-up landing – a potential crash averted only by an alert observer firing a red Very light across his bows. Not to be outdone, the squadron's ground crew made their own contribution to this litany of incidents. They skidded a lorry into a Handley Page HP.42E four-engined biplane,[22] once the pride of Imperial Airways, damaging the leading edge of one wing.

The same sorry tale continued when six aircraft were sent to Turnhouse on 20 March: 'F/O Alastair Milne Grant crashed on landing into setting sun on bogged aerodrome, no personal injury.' Then nine days later, 'F/O G.V. Proudman broke Wind Sock at S.E. corner. One plane of aircraft damaged, no personal injury.' This last episode occurred during a formation take-off. Notwithstanding the limited damage incurred – the windsock suffered more than the Spitfire – it's little wonder that Babbage's flight commander was concerned about 602's reputation for 'writing off aircraft in considerable numbers'.

In learning his trade 'Cabbage', as he inevitably became known, was more fortunate than most. Of the ten patrols and a little over 11 operational hours he flew during March, five were in company with Flying Officer Archie McKellar,[23] soon to become one of the RAF's most celebrated Battle of Britain aces. By the time he was killed on 1 November 1940, he'd been credited with at least 17 enemy aircraft destroyed. All but two of these came after he moved to No. 605 Squadron, flying Hurricanes. Equally beneficial from Babbage's perspective, those operational sorties he did fly were crammed into just 17 days, providing the continuity so important at the start of a flying career. During one of B Flight's busiest months thus far – more than 300 flying hours – the new man also accomplished the singular achievement of an incident-free first night patrol.

Unfortunately, things then got worse. In April he managed only nine operational sorties (just over nine hours' flying). It didn't help that from the middle of the month the squadron was sent north in an effort to bring them closer to the fighting: A Flight to Montrose and B Flight to Dyce. However, the 'treacherous state' of the latter airfield led to a section of three aircraft diverting to Montrose almost immediately; Dyce became temporarily 'unfit for landing Spitfires, owing to the heavy continuous rain of the last few days'. The upshot of these upheavals was that for nearly three weeks, from 5 to 24 April, Babbage did not fly a single operational sortie. It was during this time that another change occurred. A new CO, Squadron Leader George Pinkerton, arrived on 4 April to replace the recently promoted Farquhar. For Pinkerton it was a return home he'd served with 602 before.

Spending most of May at Dyce, some 90 miles north north-east of Drem, proved less than exciting for Babbage. He managed only a couple of patrols – less than two hours in the air. One of these was as part of a three-man formation, the only aircraft launched that day. Not only was there little activity – operations took place on only 12 days – those less experienced pilots who needed flying continuity the most, simply weren't able to develop the skills they'd need to survive the battle to come. It was a battle for which preparations were already in hand. On 2 May 1940 the order came to paint new markings on the squadron's aircraft: a yellow ring outside the roundels and red, white and blue vertical stripes on the tailfin. Then, with the German invasion of Belgium and Holland, on 10 May all leave was stopped and those on leave recalled. Meanwhile the squadron continued to be plagued by minor incidents. On 15 May a 'Master aircraft flew into Spitfire K9964[24] taking off. F/O McClean was uninjured.' Like so many others, this incident at Montrose could have been worse. The Master, a two-seat trainer, was carrying practice bombs which exploded on impact.

Once back at Drem, June proved little better for Babbage: just three operational patrols (three hours' flying) in the latter half of the month. One of these was only his second at night. He was not alone in finding this a challenging experience. A colleague[25] described it thus: "when you opened up to full throttle the glare from the exhaust stubs was blinding. So it was very difficult just to keep your line on the flare path . . . it was very fraught, landing was not much fun either."[26] The teenage Wellum, launched into total darkness on his first night sortie that very same month, put it another way: "It's all so confusing." So confusing, in fact, that on landing he hit the runway's Chance light[27] with his port wing, severely damaging the aircraft. Fortunate that it wasn't a write-off, he was nevertheless grounded 'indefinitely' – a sanction that later proved only temporary. After Dunkirk, which cost 92 Squadron five aircraft and their pilots, including the CO, Squadron Leader Roger Bushell,[28] the unit couldn't afford to leave anyone on the ground for long.

With the fall of France coming less than three weeks after the Dunkirk evacuation, the relative lack of activity on Babbage's own squadron is difficult to understand. As is the disproportionate amount of night flying, most of it by the squadron's most experienced crews, in a month with the longest daylight hours. The new man was more than content to leave his own contribution to such operations at a solitary one hour five minutes in the inky blackness.

As tension increased and preparations for the imminent battle continued, 7 June brought the first practice air raid drills: 'everything chaotic at first but settled down all right'. Just as well, because air raids became more common towards the end of the month. That same day Flying Officer MacLean's trials continued when his undercarriage collapsed on landing. Once again, he was fortunate: 'Not much damage, Port Wing tip and flap. Maintenance had job done and aircraft on service again in four hours.' Then on 15 June came an order to paint the undersurfaces of the squadron's aircraft duck-egg blue. Up until now they had worn a more distinctive colour scheme: the underside of one wing was painted black and the other white. The most notable event of the month came on the night of 25 June when Flight Lieutenant Johnstone, flying with the CO, shot down a He 111. It had been caught in searchlight beams and would prove the first of his several confirmed kills.[29]

July brought a marked improvement in Babbage's fortunes: 21 operational sorties and nearly 15 hours' flying – better continuity too. The discrepancy between sorties and hours reflects a preponderance of short sorties – 30 minutes or less. As activity gathered pace towards the end of the month the squadron began flying 'flap patrols' both day and night – a reaction to increased enemy activity, mainly raids by Do 17, He 111 and Ju 88 aircraft. An indication of how hard-worked the unit was becoming came on 25 July. Babbage flew a ten-minute sortie at 0640 and another of one hour 15 minutes nearly 11 hours later, landing at 1845. Then on 17 July came the appointment of yet another new CO. Pinkerton was replaced by the recently promoted Squadron Leader Sandy Johnstone. While his new boss had come to respect the young sergeant's abilities, Babbage took no part in the night patrols that were now becoming more regular.

The first month of Johnstone's command ended in familiar fashion. The ORB records:

> 'F/Lt Dunlop Urie up on flap. Heavy mist came down with the result that he piled his new aircraft. A most wonderful escape. Tore a wing clean off but managed to make a belly landing. This ground mist is going to play havoc with the Spitfires, Urie fortunately not hurt.'

Given that the demise of K9461 occurred at the end of a night sortie, 0130 on 1 August, it would perhaps be more accurate to record that the new boss's first *full* month in command began inauspiciously! As collateral for this view, Pilot Officer 'Harry' Moody 'crashed on landing' at the same time, 'in visibility of about fifty yards'. Once again, however, the pilot 'fortunately was uninjured'. While his survival, after ending up in the boundary hedge, is testament to the strength of the Spitfire's monocoque construction, the aircraft itself would never fly again.

That Johnstone would go on to enjoy considerable further success prompts a reflection on Trenchard's introduction of the auxiliaries in 1925. It presaged a change in the social make-up of the junior service – one accelerated by the prospect of conflict with Germany. But amongst the wealth and privilege of the 'weekend flyers', social acceptability was still a key consideration. It meant that before being welcomed into the fold, Johnstone had to endure a formal guest night to prove his mettle – not with throttle and stick but with knife and fork! The ability to behave well even after an evening of heavy drinking remained the mark of a gentleman. And the auxiliaries were nothing if not gentlemen.

CHAPTER 3

THE BATTLE BEGINS

IN A PURELY ARBITRARY DECISION taken after the event, the then Lord Dowding determined that the Battle of Britain began on 10 July 1940. Noted historian and chronicler of the battle, Dilip Sarkar, argues that 'if we are to accept that the Battle of Britain was fought to prevent a seaborne invasion of southern England, then surely 2 July is actually the date on which the Battle began'.[30] Two weeks earlier, in his stirring 'their finest hour' House of Commons speech of 18 June, Prime Minister Winston Churchill said he expected the Battle of Britain was 'about to begin'. Next day, for the first time, the Luftwaffe attacked Britain in force with more than 70 aircraft. It could therefore be argued that the battle began on 19 June. Such speculation apart, and acknowledging the difficulty Dowding had in determining the start date, for Cyril Babbage the Battle of Britain began in the middle of August. It was then that AOC 13 Group, required to provide reinforcements for Air Vice-Marshal Keith Park's[31] hard-pressed 11 Group, chose 602 Squadron.

In the wake of the Luftwaffe's *Adler Tag* (Eagle Day) on 13 August, Dowding decided to remove one of his hardest hit units from the front line. No. 145 Squadron had seen 11 pilots killed and two wounded in just over a month, all but one in the previous week. By then the Battle of Britain was at its height, not that Babbage and his colleagues had seen much evidence of this.

At Drem, notwithstanding the two night-landing accidents in the early hours of 1 August, the month began quietly. On several occasions operational flying was limited to just three sorties, with Babbage himself flying only two short patrols in the first 12 days: a total of just one hour and ten minutes. The only incident of note during this time came on 5 August. B Flight's Green section,[32] Flying Officer Paul Webb, Flying Officer Thomas Ritchie and Sergeant Mervyn Sprague, found a He 111 some way off the Fife coast, but it escaped into cloud before they could launch an attack.

In the absence of any other activity, rumours began circulating of a move to the south. Late on the evening of 12 August they were confirmed. The initial plan for relocation to Tangmere was changed at the last minute; Sandy Johnstone's new base would be a Tangmere satellite, Westhampnett (now Goodwood), so new that the airfield wasn't even on the map![33]

The squadron was scheduled to leave Drem early next morning, but bad weather delayed their departure. Led by the CO, 16 Spitfires eventually took off at 1200 – but not without incident. As Johnstone eased open his throttle, the station commander, Wing Commander 'Batchy' Atcherley,[34] suddenly appeared on his starboard side, his Humber staff car bouncing along the uneven surface with the burly Padre Sutherland hanging out of the rear window brandishing a set of bagpipes. Such behaviour was typical of one of the Air Force's genuine characters, a man with a mischievous sense of humour – an impressive flying background too. He was a member of the RAF's winning 1929 Schneider Trophy[35] team.

Atcherley's typically spirited performance that day was Johnstone's last impression of Drem as his aircraft 'rose into a wall of dirty black clouds'. Engine problems forced Sergeant Andy McDowell to return to base almost immediately; he would follow the next day. With Babbage flying his personal aircraft (K9839), the remaining Spitfires eventually reached Church Fenton, where they were due to refuel, albeit not without further incident. With thick unbroken cloud en route, finding the airfield proved a challenge. It was only after breaking out below, and a wide circle below 2,000ft, that a relieved

Johnstone caught sight of Spitfires on the ground. It could only be Church Fenton, he thought. Phew!

But poor weather once again delayed their departure. They finally 'left at 1610 hrs as 11 Group anxious for us to get South owing to large amount of activity. Squadron eventually arrived at West Hampnett at 1720 hrs. without further incident. A large battle was in progress at the time of landing but 602 was unable to take part because they were not on the correct R/T frequency.' They arrived to find smoke rising from a burning Me 109 nearby, while a damaged Hurricane lay marooned in the middle of the airfield. It was the mount of OC 145 Squadron, Squadron Leader John Peel,[36] who'd been forced to land his battered aircraft with no aileron control. He greeted Johnstone with his arm in a sling – the result of a bullet wound sustained on the same sortie. If Johnstone had any doubts about the task he faced in taking over from the hardest hit squadron in 11 Group, Peel soon dispelled them. Life would be difficult, witness the experience of his own brief time in command.

Shortly after his appointment, on 11 July Peel was shot down. By sheer good fortune he survived the subsequent ditching in the Channel off Selsey Bill – thanks to a coastguard who saw his aircraft go down and alerted the Selsey lifeboat. When the crew pulled him from the water he was exhausted but unhurt. In fact, he was airborne again next morning. His fortuitous rescue led to a life-long commitment to support the RNLI and a heartfelt letter of thanks to the coxswain:

> "When you arrived I had given up hope. I doubt if I could have lasted more than a few minutes. Your skill in finding me in that rough sea seems a miracle to me. You and your fellows in the Life-boat [sic] Service are doing a magnificent job."

In an engagement three days later Peel's Hurricane again sustained damage. Another crash landing followed, this time on the Isle of Wight where his aircraft overturned, putting him briefly in hospital. Such experiences were symptomatic of the losses 145 sustained during his time in command. With his squadron now down to just four aircraft and four pilots, Peel could count himself fortunate to have survived.

Next to appear was the Tangmere station (and sector) commander, Group Captain Jack Boret,[37] who'd flown with the Royal Flying Corps (RFC) in World War I, earning the MC. His airfield was home to the Hurricanes of 43 and 601 Squadrons, conveniently close to the south coast but yet to become a prime Luftwaffe target. It would first come under attack three days hence, on 16 August. Boret nevertheless confirmed that things had been 'a bit rough' recently and left Johnstone in no doubt about what to expect: up to six sorties a day plus night flying two or three times a week.

Tangmere itself, almost cheek by jowl with Westhampnett, provided traditional mess accommodation. However, half of 602's pilots found themselves living in a nearby thatched cottage, mattresses spread around on the floor. Woodcote Farm, on the edge of the airfield, served as their officers' mess. A number of airmen were billeted in a house at the Old Kennels on the Goodwood estate, whilst others were accommodated at Goodwood Golf Club. Meanwhile, some of the squadron's equipment found a home in the base of the grandstand at Goodwood racecourse. On the airfield itself, a couple of Nissen huts served as dispersals for A and B Flights. There the pilots could gaze out on a sad-looking windsock. It was one of the few markers that, like the scattering of huts, identified Tangmere's new satellite – what up until recently had been no more than three farmers' fields.

For Cyril, or 'Frank' Babbage, as he was also known, the war was about to begin in earnest. Readily identifiable by the polka-dot cravat cum scarf he always wore – a good luck present from his aunt, Gertrude Wells – in his own shy, quiet way he was determined not only to survive but to make his mark. And he would – with the help of his scarf!

The squadron's first full day at RAF Westhampnett,[38] 14 August, was one of feverish activity, albeit there was little to show for seven scrambles and more than 50 sorties: a single damaged He 111 'just west of base'. As befits a wartime boss, Sandy Johnstone led from the front, flying five times over a span of some eight hours. Babbage, meanwhile, had to content himself with just three sorties, one of only 15 minutes' duration.

He did better next day, an unusually long evening patrol of two hours. But returns from 19 sorties in three separate waves were similarly sparse – a Do 215 found 15 miles south of Portland was forced down into the sea off Ventnor – and this despite 'considerable enemy activity'. The most concentrated German effort thus far saw the Luftwaffe launch more than 2,000 sorties on 15 August, what later became known as 'the greatest day'. As so often with Battle of Britain folklore, this soubriquet owes its origins to Churchill. With news of mounting German losses, the prime minister decided to visit Dowding's Fighter Command Headquarters at Bentley Priory that day. After watching events unfold, he returned to London and declared the day one of the 'greatest in history'.[39] But history would prove him wrong. Claims of German aircraft destroyed were greatly exaggerated, as indeed were Luftwaffe claims of RAF losses – by a factor of around three in each case. The final figures on what became known in Germany as 'Black Thursday' were 75 and 34 aircraft respectively[40] – a clear victory for the RAF.

That both sides similarly and consistently overclaimed throughout the conflict is less a criticism, more a reflection on the dynamic nature of aerial combat. Sometimes involving hundreds of aircraft, the prime concern of those engaged was self-preservation rather than the ability to reconstruct life or death situations in the immediate aftermath, as required by the RAF claims process.[41]

The next 24 hours heralded a change in fortune for 602. In a remarkable sortie lasting only a minute or so, Flight Lieutenant Findlay Boyd, OC B Flight, brought down a Ju 87 'Stuka' that had just completed a bombing attack on Tangmere. Just as he took off it appeared from his left and crossed in front of him. A single burst from his guns saw it hit the ground almost intact close by. He landed immediately, and while his aircraft was being re-armed secured the first of his wartime trophies: a Luger pistol and a Leica camera. Boyd had just flown what was probably one of the shortest sorties of the war and secured what was almost certainly the quickest 'kill'.

The remainder of Boyd's formation, led by the CO and including Babbage, failed to engage the attackers. But any thirst for action was quenched by a late afternoon encounter with a large enemy formation, estimated at 60 He 111s and 30 Me 110s. Throughout a busy day the squadron claimed seven Me 110s and a single He 111 destroyed, plus a second He 111 damaged. Although Babbage missed this latter engagement, he would soon make up for it.

Despite 602's best efforts, the German raid had laid waste to Tangmere. Pilots returned to see columns of black smoke rising from damaged aircraft, and buildings turned to rubble. Worse still, some of the damaged and destroyed aircraft were from 602, sent there for servicing. At the same time on that same day, 16 August, a tragedy that would ultimately have international consequences was playing out. After his Hurricane was severely damaged in an encounter with a Ju 87, Pilot Officer 'Billy' Fiske of 601 Squadron attempted a wheels-up landing at Tangmere when his engine seized. Badly injured and burnt, he was unstrapped and pulled from the cockpit of his crashed aircraft by two ground crew. But there was little that could be done for a man who had already created his own legend. Next day, when he died in hospital, he would become the first American to be killed during the Battle of Britain.

William Meade Lindsley Fiske III was aged just 16 when he won the first of his two Olympic gold medals as a bobsleigh driver at St Moritz in 1928; the second came four years later at Lake Placid, New York. But there was no possibility of a third medal. Distaste for the Nazi regime meant he refused to compete in the 1936 Winter Olympics in Germany. Scion of a wealthy New England banking family, Fiske was an Anglophile. A graduate of Trinity College Cambridge who married the Countess of Warwick, Rose Bingham, before the war, he was also a member of London's exclusive White's Club – which was where he cemented his connection with members of 601 Squadron, 'the millionaires' squadron'. He'd been with them barely a month when he died.

On 4 July 1941, American Independence Day, a plaque commemorating Fiske, 'An American citizen who died that England might live', was unveiled in the crypt of St Paul's Cathedral by Sir Archibald Sinclair,[42] Secretary of State for Air. In a simple, moving tribute he said, "Here was a young man for whom life held much. Under no kind of compulsion he came to fight for Britain. He came and he fought and he died." The date, and indeed the tribute itself, has all the hallmarks of a prime minister keen to see America enter the fray. But this should take nothing away from Fiske's sacrifice. It seems entirely appropriate that he now lies buried in a churchyard close to Tangmere, St Mary and St Blaise, Boxgrove.

After a quiet day on 17 August – just four operational patrols, including an hour's flying for Babbage, and no contact with the Luftwaffe – the next brought a notable change of pace. 18 August would become known as 'the hardest day'. More huge raids saw Fighter Command lose 34 aircraft and the Luftwaffe 69.[43] It was a day again made famous by Churchill after visiting 11 Group's Uxbridge Headquarters. In the heat of the day, as massed German raids appeared on the plotting table, the Prime Minister was shocked when the AOC, Keith Park, revealed that he had nothing left to commit – no reserves whatsoever. Reflecting on what proved a deeply moving experience, that evening as Churchill continued on to his country residence, Chequers, he turned to his Chief of Staff, General Hastings 'Pug' Ismay,[44] with the sentiment that later came to define the Battle of Britain: words to the effect that: 'Never in the field of human conflict has so much been owed by so many to so few.' Two days later, as part of a 50-minute speech in the House of Commons, they earned their place in posterity.

Babbage flew only two short operational sorties that day, 20 and 15 minutes respectively. On the first of these he opened his account. Setting aside discrepancies between his combat report and the ORB, which itself contains inconsistencies, the action unfolded from around 1415, when the squadron took off in waves to patrol overhead base at 8,000ft. Almost immediately, they sighted a large enemy formation: 60 Ju 87s and a number of accompanying Me 109s (Babbage estimated 50–60) at 6,000ft preparing to bomb the nearby airfield at Ford. As 602's pilots headed off the first two waves of bombers and chased them out to sea, they were themselves attacked by the Me 109s. In the dogfights that followed they claimed six Ju 87s and two Me 109s destroyed, a Ju 87 probable and another six damaged. On the debit side, Flight Lieutenant Urie was wounded in the legs – they were 'full of shrapnel' – as was Flying Officer Ian Ferguson during a crash landing where he was temporarily blinded. The problem was caused by a huge flash that accompanied the severing of four out of six 33,000-volt high-tension cables. Both officers were hospitalised.

Meanwhile, of the five Spitfires 'lost', two would eventually prove repairable. One of the write-offs, Urie's X4110, provided a possibly unique statistic. Its total service life amounted to less than 30 minutes. Earlier, when Urie was ordered airborne, he arrived at his own aircraft to find it on jacks with no wheels. Undeterred, he jumped into a newly delivered Spitfire, a replacement for one of the four lost two days earlier. It had no squadron markings, neither had its guns been harmonised, but he had little choice. In any event, it mattered not because he soon found himself under attack and effectively left for dead by his Me 109 assailant. Had it not been for the armour plating behind his seat, Urie's injuries could have been much worse.

One of the Ju 87s fell to Babbage's eight .303 Browning machine guns. As the Stuka tried to escape out to sea at about 200ft, he attacked from directly astern. While the German pilot sideslipped furiously to frustrate Babbage's aim, his rear gunner opened up on his Spitfire pursuer. A quick two-second burst silenced the German's own 7.92mm machine gun, allowing Babbage to reposition for another six seconds of fire. It was enough to send his prey crashing into the sea. As he headed back towards land, he was surprised to see an Me 109 flash almost directly overhead. His first thoughts, as he turned hard to pursue the Luftwaffe fighter, were that he'd probably had a narrow escape. No matter. By his quick reactions he'd created an opportunity for an attack. Pressing hard on the gun button he saw part of a hopeful three-second burst impact on the German aircraft's fuselage before it disappeared from sight at around 1,000ft. Out of ammunition now after firing 2,400 rounds, he had little option but to return to base. His first encounter with the enemy had lasted barely 20 minutes – it felt a lot less – and brought both a confirmed and a damaged.[45] But there was no time to celebrate. A change of aircraft and he was airborne again just 35 minutes later. Sergeant Cyril Babbage would always remember Sunday 18 August 1940, the day he opened his wartime account.

The squadron's short-notice departure from Drem left them initially with only limited engineering and administrative support – all that could be prioritised into a couple of Harrow bomber-turned-transport aircraft – so the arrival by road of the remainder of 602 in the early hours of 19 August was more than welcome. It was a sentiment reinforced by the fact that what had initially been planned as a temporary assignment to Westhampnett had now been made permanent. Unique in the annals of 11 Group, only two enemy aircraft were claimed that day: Ju 88s, both by 602, one in the morning and one later in the day – a victory in which Babbage claimed a quarter share. If that was the good news, the bad was that Harry Moody was shot down for the second time in two days, forced to bail out once again after his aircraft caught fire.

The next five days were relatively quiet for Babbage – regular flying, mainly short sorties of less than an hour, but little action. There were few operational patrols and it wasn't until 23 August that the squadron again sighted the enemy: a single Ju 88 that escaped. The only incident of note occurred that same day when Thomas Ritchie collided with a Spitfire from another squadron. He was fortunate not to sustain any major damage and landed safely; the other aircraft was lost but the pilot bailed out unharmed. After all the excitement that followed *Adler Tag*, these few days represented something of a lull; it was almost as if the Luftwaffe was licking its wounds. That wasn't the case though. Manston in particular was being hit hard – as were Kenley, Debden, Hornchurch and North Weald. But it wasn't just the airfields that were suffering; it was Park's fighters and their crews.

For 602 Squadron, the battle began again in earnest on 25 August. Babbage flew twice that day. His second sortie was in the early evening, part of a squadron scramble to intercept 'large numbers of enemy aircraft' crossing the coast between Swanage and Portland. Almost immediately they sighted 'a solid mass of enemy aircraft at 15,000ft between Dorchester and the coast'; numbers were estimated at 200–300 Do 17s, Me 109s and Me 110s. In the major engagement that followed, Flying Officer 'Bill' Coverley[46] and Sergeant Sprague bailed out safely, the latter over the sea where he was fortunate to be picked up by a Walrus, none the worse for his experience. It proved to be a good day for the squadron: a haul of six Me 110s, three Me 109s and three Do 17s destroyed, plus a probable Me 109. Cyril Babbage claimed two more of these German scalps.

When he engaged the enemy formation there was no shortage of targets. It's a measure of his growing ability that he was the only one to break through to the bombers that represented the primary threat. In doing so he found himself almost head-on with an Me 110 – hardly the best angle to attack because it brought into play the German fighter-bomber's own potent armament.[47] Recognising that the advantage lay with him – he was some 10–15 degrees off the German's fore-and-aft axis – he closed to around 100 yards, loosing off a three-second burst. The effect was astonishing. The 110's cockpit collapsed in a shower of plexiglass, it flipped over onto its back and disappeared in a sheet of flames. As Babbage broke away to avoid the debris, almost immediately he latched on to the tail of a Do 17, slightly below him at 14,000ft and heading for home. A six-second burst, closing from 250 to around 80 yards hit home. His attack destroyed the upper gun turret and damaged the German's starboard engine; it was pouring smoke. As the bomber turned back towards land, Babbage launched another attack, a virtual repeat of the first, which finished the job. His four-second burst saw the bomber half-roll, drop like a stone and crash into the sea. Ammunition gone – he'd fired over 2,000 rounds – it was time to return to the safety of Westhampnett. As he did so he replayed in his mind an astonishing minute or two. It was surreal. One moment he was part of a whirling melee of aircraft, deafened almost by the rattle of his machine guns, and the next heading quietly back to base with nothing but the comforting sound of his Merlin engine to keep him company.

Babbage's combat report on this encounter concludes with a chilling sentence: 'One of E/A crew attempted to bail out and I killed him during second burst.' Here was the harsh face of reality – the human side of the deadly game played out in the skies above the south-east almost every day. It was Flying Officer Henry Cranebook's role, as the squadron intelligence officer, to collate such reports – no easy task dealing with youngsters who minutes ago had been fighting for their lives, but it was one in which he was very much in his element. Did he think to question the use of such emotive language? Probably not. There was little sign of modern sensitivities then. All Cranebrook needed were the facts to substantiate a claim. Recalling the events of that summer 50 years later, Geoffrey Wellum's 92 Squadron mentor, Brian Kingcome,[48] captured succinctly the situation in which Babbage found himself: "nerves at full stretch in a deadly dance of death when split-second timing separated the killers from the killed."[49]

In the minds of many of those who took part, aerial combat was a case of machine against machine rather than man against man. This was particularly so during the Battle of Britain where later, in accordance with Park's instructions, it often boiled down to Hurricanes versus the bombers with Spitfires pitted against the accompanying fighters. Brian Kingcome again:

> ". . . closing on the bombers too fast for the escorting fighters to reach us in time, straight through the bomber formation firing short bursts

> at opportunity targets, the sound of our guns like tearing calico, then turning to meet the fighter escort diving down from above, too late to protect the bombers from the first scything attack. The vicious aerial brawl, fighter versus fighter . . ."[50]

While few saw the struggle as personal, Babbage's flight commander, Findlay Boyd, was known for his hatred of the Germans. The same was true of the Poles, of course, for whom invasion and defeat inspired a justifiable animus. After the battle, Dowding singled out for special praise the 'unsurpassed gallantry' of their squadrons and the contribution they made to the outcome of the battle.

On 26 August Babbage again flew twice. His second take-off came at 1610 when the squadron was scrambled to intercept another huge raid approaching from the south at 15,000ft: 150 He 111s, Do 17s and Me 109s. It led to a major skirmish over Selsey Bill where 602 claimed three He 111s, a Do 17 and a probable Me 109. But they paid the penalty. Flying Officer Hector MacLean was seriously wounded and eventually lost a foot after crash landing at Tangmere. And Cyril Babbage was shot down. More fortunate than his colleague, he bailed out unharmed and was quickly rescued.

Before recounting the tale of the young sergeant's demise – and his subsequent good fortune – there's a brief, surprising postscript to 602 Squadron's operations on this extraordinary day. Later in the evening, Flying Officers Webb and Jack claimed a He 59 floatplane around 20 miles off St Catherine's Point, the southern tip of the Isle of Wight; it was 'possibly picking up survivors from the battle earlier in the afternoon'. Although they bore red cross markings, these obsolescent biplanes were seen as legitimate targets. They were said to indulge in more than just rescue missions, reporting on shipping and coastal installations and were often supported by Me 109s – which was why Webb and Jack were keen to destroy the intruder quickly, before any fighter cover arrived.

Babbage's fateful sortie was the last he would fly during the busiest month thus far in his fledgling operational career; his next would be on 8 September, by which time the nature of the battle would have changed. Time to reflect not just on his lucky escape, but also on his early successes. Rated now as 'above average', he'd proved himself both a skilful pilot and an able marksman. Equally if not more important, he seemed blessed with more than his share of luck, which was never a bad thing.

In terms of aerial combat, it was those who learned fastest who survived. And Babbage learned quickly. One of the earliest lessons he absorbed was that it's one thing to manoeuvre into a firing position, but even in the target-rich environment in which he sometimes found himself, it was another thing altogether to hit a turning, jinking opponent desperate to survive. That said, any number of crews on both sides were shot down whilst flying straight and level, blissfully unaware of the danger from directly astern – the easiest position from which to secure a kill. All it took was a matter of seconds. The more difficult the target, the closer a pilot needed to be for his rounds to strike home. And Babbage had shown himself willing to approach perilously close to his targets. This was dangerous on two counts: it presented bomber gunners with an easier shot, and it brought the added risk of flying through debris.

It didn't help the less accomplished pilots that Fighter Command practice was to harmonise guns at 400 yards. This was the range at which an aircraft's cone of fire was at its most concentrated. Knowing how difficult it was for the average pilot to hold his gunsight on a target long enough at such a range to provide a lethal burst of fire, Squadron Leader 'Sailor' Malan,[51] an excellent shot himself, had 74 Squadron's guns harmonised at 250 yards. In fact, he encouraged his pilots to get even closer. The first of his ten 'Rules for Air Fighting' began, 'Wait until you see the whites of his eyes . . .'. Babbage would almost certainly have read this entreaty – if not by then, certainly after the battle. Eventually, Malan's ten commandments were pinned up in almost every dispersal hut.

The foregoing digression is necessary background to Babbage's demise and puts his 20-minute excursion on 26 August into context. As he climbed towards the phalanx of enemy aircraft late that afternoon he lost contact with his leader. Almost the first thing he saw as he entered the fray was a pair of Me 109s attacking another Spitfire which plainly needed help. (It turned out to be Pilot Officer Ellis Aries, a recent arrival, young and inexperienced but already with a Heinkel to his credit.) Babbage quickly manoeuvred astern the German wingman, whose attention was elsewhere, and pressed the gun button: a five-second burst, starting at 250 yards and closing to 150. It was enough to force the German fighter to break off his own attack. As he turned away, Babbage turned inside him, leading the turn, and took a difficult deflection shot. His second attack saw the enemy fighter flick into a spin, its engine belching black smoke.

With so many potential targets around him – the upside of being vastly outnumbered – there was no point in chasing after an aircraft that was plainly doomed. Better to turn his attention to the 15–20 enemy bombers heading back to France. Selecting the centre Do 215[52] of a three-aircraft vic formation, he opened fire from 300 yards directly astern and closed until he ran out of ammunition. His rounds struck home but there were no obvious signs of damage. To escape the heavy crossfire from his target's companions, Babbage then broke away down and to the left. The next thing he knew was that he'd been hit by three cannon shells. They had to have come from an Me 109. But he'd been lucky; it could have been closer – fatal even. In no time his aircraft was on fire. There was no option but to put his trust in the Irvin parachute that had served many of his colleagues so well and consign his Spitfire, X4188, to a watery grave.

The next thing he remembered was the crack, accompanied by a jerk, as his parachute opened. He'd rarely seen such a reassuring sight.

CHAPTER 4

MAYER-AST, HAUPTMANN HANS-KARL MAYER

BABBAGE WAS SHOT DOWN BY Hauptmann Hans-Karl Mayer of 1/JG53,[53] a Luftwaffe *Experte* nicknamed Mayer-Ast. Tall as a tree (*Ast* translates as branch or bough), it was a matter of some amazement to his Staffel (squadron) that he ever managed to lever himself into the cramped cockpit of an Me 109. On 3 September, eight days after his latest victory, he would be awarded the coveted *Ritterkreuz des Eisernen Kreuzes*, the Knight's Cross.[54]

Established by Hitler on 1 September 1939, the Knight's Cross was the Luftwaffe equivalent of 'the Blue Max', the *Pour le Mérite* made famous during World War I. The latter owed its nickname in part to the insignia: a blue-enamelled Maltese cross. Amongst notable members of the *Luftstreitkräfte*, the German Army Air Service, honoured with the award were Max Immelmann and Oswald Boelcke (the first two recipients), together with Manfred von

Richthofen, 'the Red Baron', and Hermann Göring. As for the Knight's Cross in World War II, the criterion for the award was a specific number of aerial victories – a figure that increased in each case as the conflicts progressed. With the abdication of Kaiser Wilhelm II on 9 November 1918, just two days before the Armistice, signalling the end of the Prussian monarchy, the *Pour le Mérite* would never again be awarded, although recipients could continue to wear it.

Progressively higher grades of the Knight's Cross were introduced at regular intervals as the war continued: with oak leaves, with oak leaves and swords, with oak leaves, swords and diamonds and, finally, with golden oak leaves, swords and diamonds – albeit this last award went to Göring alone. As with the Blue Max, recipients were required to wear it as a neck decoration whenever in uniform. With each award personally approved by the Führer, it led to intense competition for recognition between Luftwaffe Experten. As the Battle of Britain drew to a close this culminated in a race between Adolf Galland, Werner Mölders and Helmut Wick. When Wick was killed, on 28 November 1940, he was disputing the lead in a battle which, for the British ended nearly a month earlier, on 31 October. But from a German perspective, the *Luftschlacht um England* lasted from *Adler Tag* until Operation Barbarossa, the invasion of Russia on 22 June 1941. Mölders was the first airman in history to reach the 100 mark but was killed on 22 November 1941 when the He 111 in which he was a passenger crashed: a landing accident at Breslau. Ironically, he was en route to the funeral of World War I ace Ernst Udet. Galland survived the war, ending with 104 enemy aircraft to his name – all on the Western Front.

If the German view of Battle of Britain timescales differed from the British, so too did the respective air forces' approach to individual achievement in the air. It wasn't just the discrepancy in the number of kills, where Luftwaffe Experten considerably outscored the top RAF aces, it was also the manner in which the former pursued their goals. As the battle wore on, personal success sometimes appeared to count for more than collective achievement. The individual seemed more important than the team, which did little for morale at a time when the RAF increasingly held the upper hand. This takes us back to late November and Wick's demise. As he pursued his ambitions, those he flew with were tasked with protecting him – to the detriment of any firing opportunities that might come their way, thereby increasing their own vulnerability. (In a practice capable of misinterpretation, the names of lost colleagues were sometimes recorded on an aircraft. This was in addition to the tailfin markers recording a pilot's victories.)

Notwithstanding those RAF pilots accorded ace status, the supreme accolade, particularly as the war progressed and the service went on the offensive, was airborne leadership, the art of protecting rather than sacrificing a No. 2. It was the stock in trade of men like Brian Kingcome and Jamie Rankin.[55] The latter, Wing Commander Flying at Biggin Hill in 1942, "played the air war like a chess board . . . In command of every situation, [he] exuded a confidence that engendered an unshakable sense of security in every pilot who flew with him. He was universally respected and admired."[56]

By the time Babbage encountered Mayer, the German had 15 victories to his credit,[57] plus eight more claimed with the Condor Legion during the Spanish Civil War. Not only was he up against a vastly more experienced pilot, in the Me 109 he faced an aircraft that was in some ways superior to his Mk 1 Spitfire – certainly in terms of top speed and in a steep dive.

The Me 109 was more than a match for most of the aircraft Mayer encountered during the battle for France. His victims on 14 May 1940, the day he joined the small coterie of fighter pilots who became an 'ace in a day', included only a single fighter, a Hurricane; the others were Blenheims and Battles.

Babbage would not only survive this close encounter, he would survive the war too. But Mayer was on borrowed time; he had less than two months to live. On 17 October 1940, again flying the latest version Me 109 E-7, he was shot down – in all likelihood by a 222 Squadron Spitfire, that of either Flying Officer Desmond McMullen or Sergeant John Burgess. His body was washed ashore ten days later at Littlestone, in Kent. Initially it was impossible to identify him other than by his rank, so he was buried in the cemetery at RAF Hawkinge as an unknown Hauptmann. Once the 29-year-old was properly identified his headstone was engraved accordingly, albeit not as Hans-Karl but as Hans Carl Mayer. It remains there to this day, a mark of the respect accorded to such individuals, worthy opponents.

Babbage's arrival on the beach near Bognor pier caused quite a stir. Because it had been anticipated, there was a sizeable reception party there to greet the fortunate airman: fortunate not to have been wounded, fortunate too to have been rescued so quickly. He had no dinghy, just a Mae West, and there was no air-sea rescue (ASR) system at the time. Survival – rescue – in such circumstances was simply a matter of luck during the Battle of Britain. It would be well into 1941 before ASR flights, equipped with Lysanders (and later a few Ansons), began to form along the coast to act as search aircraft for the boats that were the only rescue vessels – the odd Walrus apart.

It was Babbage's good fortune not only to be shot down relatively close to the coast, but also to be seen bailing out by some fishermen. They watched the crazy, spiralling descent of his damaged aircraft until it impacted the sea, throwing up plumes of water and briefly adding a foaming splash of white to the otherwise grey surface. Then, turning their attention to the progress of his parachute as it drifted gently downwards, they set off in their motorboat to rescue the downed pilot. Not knowing what condition he would be in, they feared the worst. But they needn't have worried. Babbage had been remarkably lucky.

Others too had been following the unfolding drama. It meant that the drenched pilot's eventual arrival on Bognor beach was marked by a welcoming committee of officers in uniform, soldiers, police, civilians and a local photographer. The resulting images, poignant and dramatic, captured the spirit of the moment: hands were shaken, congratulations offered and a proffered cigarette gratefully lit.

Babbage was eventually taken to Bognor Regis War Memorial Hospital. Two days later he was discharged, none the worse for wear. He owed his return to Westhampnett to his CO. Together with the squadron medic, 'Doc' Willey,[58] Sandy Johnstone arrived at the hospital to find 'the gallant sergeant' fit to be discharged, albeit his clothing was still damp. Wearing an overcoat borrowed from a hospital porter, he was promptly bundled into a car and delivered safely back to the sergeants' mess.

Johnstone and the Doc had previously visited another hospital-bound pilot, Flying Officer MacLean at the Royal West Sussex. Babbage had been fortunate, less so his colleague. MacLean never saw the Me 109 that raked his aircraft with cannon fire then flashed past, out of ammunition or fuel he assumed, as it headed back to France in the wake of returning He 111s. Alone now in the sky over the Channel, as he turned his damaged aircraft back towards the coast all he knew was immense pain. Glancing down, he saw blood on his legs – less on the left than the right, which seemed in a terrible mess. Little did he realise that his right foot had been detached. The resultant loss of blood was making him nauseous, but he could still think clearly enough to improvise a tourniquet and realise that bailing out simply wasn't an option. In severe pain and with the controls barely functioning, he knew he had to make landfall soon. With Tangmere closer than Westhampnett, it was there that he crash-landed.

It seemed an age before the rescue services arrived, by which time MacLean had extricated himself from his wrecked aircraft.[59] All that remained inside was a severed foot, clothed frustratingly from MacLean's viewpoint in a brand-new boot. Strapped onto a stretcher with a proper tourniquet applied, he was rushed to hospital where his right leg was amputated below the knee. It brought to an end his flying career, but not his time in the RAF. As a footnote (no pun intended) to another remarkable escape, MacLean eventually retired as a wing commander with two shared bombers to his credit, albeit his leg continued to pain him in later life as a solicitor.

Nearly 50 years later, an eyewitness account of Babbage's shooting-down emerged. It makes a fascinating story. In the late 1980s a postcard collector from Northants, a Mr Savory, purchased a group of five postcards from a local fair. Keen to discover their provenance and led to believe they depicted Battle of Britain events in the Littlehampton area, Savory wrote to the editor of the *West Sussex Gazette* with a plea for help. On 21 May 1987 nearly half a page was dedicated to his quest. Readers' responses revealed that four out of the five postcards referred to an incident involving a crashed German bomber at Pagham, near Bognor, while the fifth showed 'Sgt Cyril F. Babbage returning to shore'. One respondent forwarded a clipping from an unidentified newspaper that described the event:

> "A thrilling air battle was witnessed over a South-East Coast town on Monday afternoon during an air raid alarm, when machine-gun fire

> rattled overhead, and the thuds of bombs were heard exploding in the distance, punctuated by sharp cracks of anti-aircraft guns . . . As soon as our ground defences held their fire nothing could be heard except the sharp rat-tat of machine guns . . . One of our fighter pilots during the engagement bailed out of his plane and could be seen descending towards the sea. He pitched in the sea about half a mile off shore, where he was picked up by some fishermen. He was brought ashore with cheers ringing in his ears from several hundred persons who flocked to the sea-shore, although the all-clear had not sounded, thus incidentally, exposing themselves to extreme danger."

The fishermen who brought Babbage ashore were from Littlehampton; the 'L.I.' identifier on their boat explains the original dealer's attribution. The rescuers, 'Messrs N. & A. Ide and a member of the Ragless family', recalled that Babbage was smiling cheerfully – he'd just shot down a Messerschmitt prior to two others setting upon him over Selsey Bill. The last record of this postcard and its iconic picture is of its sale at auction in 2015.[60] The original photograph was published in a national newspaper, attributed to Frank L'Alouette, a Bognor photographer, and titled 'One of our pilots is safe'.

There's a final, tragic footnote to Babbage's Bognor story. He became good friends with one of the soldiers who helped him from the boat that day. They often arranged to meet in London during the young sergeant's occasional periods of leave. After one such evening together, his friend was killed while driving back to Aldershot – his car struck by a stray German bomb. To Babbage the survivor, it seemed a cruel quirk of fate. He was devastated.

After the events of 26 August, and the interest and excitement they generated, the remainder of the month proved relatively quiet for the squadron. There was only limited flying on the next two days, with no operational patrols, and this despite a spell of hot, dry weather. It was much the same on 29 August; there were no engagements during five patrols – likewise the three flown the following day. Then, on 31 August, there was action at last. Scrambled to patrol between Biggin Hill and Gravesend, the squadron engaged 28 Ju 88s escorted by some 60 Me 109s. The destruction of a Ju 88 and a Me 109, plus two more 'possible' 109s, was a satisfactory return for a single damaged Spitfire. That said, the coining of a new term in the ORB, a 'possible', smacks rather of wishful thinking.

As he recovered from his ordeal, it seemed that Babbage wasn't missing much excitement. This isn't to trivialise the life-or-death situations in which he and his colleagues regularly found themselves. Rather it's to highlight the stimulus, the adrenaline rush, that engagement with the enemy brought to tired bodies.

CHAPTER 5

A CHANGE OF TACTICS

In Babbage's continued temporary absence – he was granted R&R, leave to 'rest and recuperate' – September began quietly for 602 Squadron.

Few operational patrols were flown in the first five days of the month. There was only one action of any consequence. On 4 September a scramble resulted in the interception of a large enemy formation: 40 Do 17s escorted by 15–20 Me 110s. In the resulting exchange, one involving a number of Me 109s too, the squadron destroyed two Do 17s, an Me 109 and an Me 110, while a Do 17 and an Me 110 were claimed as probables and another Me 110 as damaged. And all this for the loss of just a single Spitfire.

More was to follow, with an encounter on 6 September that Babbage did well to miss. The ORB records that '"B" Flight was surprised by Me.109s, whose presence had not been noted, and suffered severely, 3 Spitfires being destroyed for 1 Me.109 on the enemy's side. P/O Ritchie was slightly injured.'

With events set to take a dramatic turn, it's worth considering for a moment the stage the Battle of Britain had now reached. The Luftwaffe had been making steady progress in its efforts to destroy Fighter Command both in the air and on the ground – aircraft and pilots too. The situation was summed up well by Sandy Johnstone: "... we are losing too many aircraft for comfort, although Supermarines [sic] are pulling out all the stops to make good our losses. Regretfully they cannot turn out pilots to match."[61] Had German intelligence been better – the important role of sector stations like Tangmere was simply not appreciated – and had the Luftwaffe known just how difficult things had become for Fighter Command as they targeted airfields, Göring might not have made what amounted to a strategic blunder.

Saturday 7 September was arguably the turning point in the Battle of Britain – the day that the Luftwaffe discarded a potentially winning strategy and changed the focus of its attacks to centres of population, mainly London. Thus began the Blitz. During the next eight months, until the night of 10/11 May 1941, the UK's civilian population would be subjected to unprecedented levels of attack by day and by night. It would result in the loss of around 43,000 civilian lives – nearly half the total civilian fatalities during the entire war – some 30,000 in London alone. More than 1.1 million houses and flats would be damaged or destroyed and one London family in six would lose their home.

It wasn't until around 1600 that day that it became clear to those at Fighter Command's Bentley Priory Headquarters that things had changed. Radar detected a massive raid forming up over the Pas-de-Calais and soon the Observer Corps was reporting hundreds of aircraft approaching the Kent coast. By 1630 every fighter squadron within reasonable proximity of London was either airborne or on readiness. With Tangmere close to the coast, 602 Squadron's Spitfires, closely followed by the Hurricanes of 43 Squadron, were amongst the first to make contact with this massive raid on the capital. The ORB notes that 602 Squadron 'at 18,000 feet sighted 28 Do.17's escorted by 100 Me.109's'. This hardly does justice to the overall size of the raid: some 350 bombers escorted by over 600 fighters[62] en route for the Docklands. Johnstone had 'never seen so many aircraft in the air at one time. It was awe-inspiring'. Near Staines he saw ten waves of Do 17s bearing down on London. He attacked four of these but in the action that followed, most of it over Kent, four Spitfires were lost, including those of Flying Officer Coverley and Pilot Officer Moody, who were both reported missing. Against this, the squadron destroyed a Do 17, an Me 109 and an Me 110; two Me 109s were counted as probables, while a Ju 88 and He 111 were claimed as damaged.

It later emerged that Harry Moody disappeared over Biggin Hill, but no trace was ever found of either his aircraft or his body. Bill Coverley was seen engaged with an Me 109 when he was shot down in flames, again near Biggin Hill. He was thought to have bailed out, but it would be more than a week before his body was found. Meanwhile Pilot Officer 'Pedro' Hanbury[63] limped back to Westhampnett, his aircraft trailing black smoke. He'd been lucky to survive a first operational encounter where he damaged a Do 17 before falling foul of the fighter cover. Pilot Officer Ellis Aries, his aircraft similarly damaged, force-landed in a field near Wrotham, not far from Maidstone. He would fly only once more during the battle, on 14 September, whereupon he was grounded for health reasons.[64]

It turned out that 602 was not the only unit to suffer that day. 43 Squadron lost three Hurricanes with two pilots killed, 234 Squadron lost two Spitfires together with their pilots, while 249 Squadron from North Weald lost six Hurricanes (one possibly to 'friendly' anti-aircraft fire) with one pilot killed and three wounded.[65] For the civilian population, worse was to come. When night fell another German raid arrived to find the docks still ablaze. London had just experienced the first of 57 consecutive days and nights of bombardment.

Ever conscious of the dangers they faced in the air, the pilots of 602 Squadron were now starkly aware of the plight of their civilian counterparts, those housed in England's capital. It seemed that CAS, Air Chief Marshal Sir Cyril Newall, had chosen an inopportune time to visit the squadron. Listening to crews debrief in the early evening, he could barely believe what he was hearing and soon hastened back to London to assess the damage for himself.

Babbage was delighted to climb back into a familiar cockpit again next day – excited too, truth be told. August had been busy: 24 operational sorties and more than 19 hours' flying during which he secured four confirmed victories and a share in another. But he was about to embark on one of the most demanding periods of his short operational career. That said, his return to flying on 8 September was anything but typical; he took part in the second of two brief, uneventful three-man patrols – just 30 minutes' flying. A break in the weather, cloud and rain, led to a day of strictly limited operations.

After the previous day's losses there was welcome news with the arrival of three new pilots, including a 19-year-old who would become one of the RAF's most ebullient and colourful characters: Pilot Officer 'Paddy' Barthropp,[66] "an easy-going, devil-may-care fellow who rarely took anything seriously – certainly no one in authority".[67] Like Babbage, he missed the main action of the day on 9 September. Engagements with mixed bomber formations and their fighter cover resulted in claims of a Ju 88, a Do 17, a Do 215 and two Me 109s destroyed, a probable Do 17 and a damaged Me 109. In terms of losses, both the newly promoted Flight Lieutenant Webb and Sergeant 'Ginger' Whall were forced to crash land their damaged aircraft. Webb was fortunate to survive a fearsome, high-speed crash that sheared off both wings and saw the tail section break away before the nose of his Spitfire buried itself in soft ground. Remarkably, his only injuries were a broken wrist, four broken fingers and a deep cut to his forehead. Whall was even more fortunate. He suffered only minor injuries and would resume flying on 18 September. Even more remarkably, his aircraft, N3282, would be flying again late next day.[68]

To explain Barthropp's immediate entry into the fray, unlike Babbage he arrived qualified (but by no means experienced) on the Spitfire. He'd been flying Hectors with 613 Squadron when he volunteered for Fighter Command and before arriving at Westhampnett he benefited from a short Spitfire conversion course at No. 7 OTU. He would spend only three months with 602 before moving to 91 Squadron, during which time he would claim two shared enemy bombers destroyed and a further damaged.[69] Shot down and captured in May 1942, Barthropp spent the next three years as a prisoner of war (POW), including 18 months in Stalag Luft III, 100 days of which were in solitary confinement for various misdemeanours. Scheduled to take part in the Great Escape in March 1944, he was fortunate that 'Harry' was discovered before he could enter the tunnel. Of the 76 who did escape, 73 were recaptured – 50 of whom were summarily executed, murdered by the Gestapo.

The arrival of new pilots like Barthropp was significant in another way. The squadrons that did best, that suffered fewest losses and achieved the highest kill:loss ratio during the battle, were the most experienced units. But as the struggle stretched beyond the long summer days and losses mounted, battle-hardened crews were at a premium. It forced Dowding to introduce a stabilisation scheme whereby squadrons were designated 'A', 'B' or 'C' category, based on levels of pilot experience. 'A' units, those with the highest levels of trained crews, he reserved mainly for 11 Group and its neighbouring stations. 'B' squadrons were also kept up to strength but designated as reliefs, while 'C' category units were allowed only five or six experienced pilots to train the neophytes. While 602 was designated 'A' and remained in situ, 601 and 43 Squadrons were replaced at Tangmere by 213 and 607 Squadrons.

A final word on the level of losses that drove these decisions: in the period 25 August to 2 September, 616 Squadron lost five pilots and 12 aircraft. Between 25 August and 5 September, 603 Squadron lost 12 pilots and 16 aircraft and during a similar period 253 Squadron's losses were nine pilots and 13 aircraft.[70] Such losses were plainly unsustainable, suggesting that the Luftwaffe's change of tactics on 7 September could hardly have come at a better time for Fighter Command. That said, it further exposed Dowding's main weakness: inadequate defences against night raids. For the pilots of 602 Squadron the extent to which this had a bearing on the events of 10 September is impossible to say. But it did highlight another of Dowding's concerns, the sheer exhaustion – cumulative tiredness – affecting his crews.

With daylight fast disappearing that Tuesday evening, A Flight's Red section was ordered airborne and kept aloft by the Tangmere sector controller until long after dark. This was despite a prior warning from Sandy Johnstone that the pilots concerned were not 'fully night trained'. His caution was ignored and, unfortunately, all three came to grief. Sergeant Elcome crashed into a tree on Bognor golf course and was concussed, while Flying Officer 'Mickey' Mount and Pilot Officer Pedro Hanbury damaged their aircraft attempting to land at Tangmere – their only option given that Westhampnett wasn't equipped for night flying. Even more worrying, these accidents would leave the squadron with only eight serviceable aircraft next day. Babbage, with limited night experience himself (just a couple of sorties, the most recent at the end of June) was fortunate to miss the carnage. In his accustomed position as a member of Green section, he flew a short patrol earlier in the day.

There's more to these night accidents than meets the eye. Mount was on his fourth sortie of a long day. His crash landing came nearly 15 hours after he launched on his first sortie of the morning. Notwithstanding the catnaps between flights that were the norm, tiredness was inevitably taking its toll. Pilots sometimes found themselves flying up to five times a day. Add to this the pressure of no-notice scrambles, regular combat and the struggle to survive, and the cumulative effect was potentially debilitating. The new boys had been warned, of course – witness Jack Boret's cautionary words on Johnstone's arrival at Westhampnett less than a month earlier. He had warned that life would be tough. But it would be another two weeks before the CO faced up to this reality.

To conclude discussion of these events on a more positive note, Sandy Johnstone had earlier received better news. He was genuinely delighted to learn of the award of a DFM to Sergeant Ginger Whall, 'a fellow who says very little and gets on with his job without fuss and bother'.[71] Such individuals – Babbage was in the same mould – were the very bedrock of a successful squadron.

With aircraft numbers dwindling, Babbage was fortunate to fly twice on 11 September. His second sortie was late afternoon when, together with the Hurricanes of 213 Squadron, 602's eight remaining Spitfires were vectored towards a formation of 20–30 Do 17s accompanied by a similar number of Me 110s and a few Me 109s. He soon found himself at the heart of the action, chasing an Me 110 that had broken away to the south. Attacking from directly abeam, about 500ft above, he fired a three-second burst, closing from 250 to 100 yards. But it wasn't decisive; there was no obvious effect. As he broke away, he watched the 110 head into the sun, positioning for an attack of its own. As he turned towards the potential threat the two of them met almost head-on at the same height. Careful to avoid his opponent's direct line of fire (he'd been in this situation before!), Babbage closed rapidly from 400 to 150 yards while loosing off a one-and-a-half second burst. Self-preservation then kicked in and he broke away high and to the left, using the sun as cover while he positioned for another beam attack.

This time he was successful. A three-second burst from 250 down to 100 yards saw his victim enter a 45-degree dive. At medium level by now, and convinced he was alone, he risked following the 110 down until it crashed into the sea. He then paid the penalty for climbing back up to 16,000ft, where he was attacked by two more Me 110s. He managed to squeeze off a few rounds at one of them, again from almost head-on, before escaping their attention and heading back to base. He'd fired 1,250 rounds in all – about half his ammunition. As testament to the dangers of these sort of attacks, after landing he found that his aircraft had sustained damage to the starboard wing. He wasn't aware that he had been hit. Fortunately, the damage was relatively minor and X4269 was flying again three days later.

Babbage's Spitfire may have survived the day, but three others were lost. Missing too, assumed lost, was Sergeant Sprague; no one had seen him go down. Pilot Officer Nigel Rose meanwhile was 'slightly wounded'. The squadron's claims amounted to an Me 109, two Me 110s and a 'Jaguar' (a modified Ju 88 according to the CO)[72] destroyed, plus a probable Me 109 and damaged Jaguar. There's a sad footnote to the loss of Mervyn Sprague. Posted missing just four days after returning from honeymoon, it was not until nearly a month later that his body was found. After he failed to return, his new wife visited the airfield every day, sitting in a car for hours on end, staring in vain at the B Flight dispersal hut. Sprague's was not the only wartime marriage to be cut tragically short, of course. A similar fate would later befall one of his erstwhile colleagues, Pedro Hanbury, killed when the Hudson in which he was a passenger was shot down over the Bay of Biscay on 3 June 1943; he'd been married just 12 days. One piece of better news did emerge that day though: Sandy Johnstone had been awarded a DFC.

There was little to excite 602 in general or Babbage in particular over the next few days, although he continued to fly regularly, accumulating hours that added to his overall experience. The Blitz had changed things for those at Tangmere. They would change again on the day destined to be celebrated as Battle of Britain Day. If things went wrong on 7 September, with Keith Park away from his headquarters, on Sunday 15 September almost everything went right for the man who managed events hour-by-hour, doing more than any other single individual to secure victory.

CHAPTER 6

A SPECIAL SUNDAY

As Babbage sat relaxing in the B Flight dispersal hut, not long after dawn on what would turn into a beautiful late summer's day, there was no obvious sign of what was to come. But 15 September 1940 would later prove one of Fighter Command's busiest days. As an uncharacteristically quiet morning wore on, he was blissfully unaware that the plotters at Fighter Command Headquarters were seeing a major raid building over the Pas-de-Calais. Park, meanwhile, was biding his time. Better to engage the enemy over southern England where his precious assets, Spitfire and Hurricane pilots, stood a better chance of returning to action should they be shot down – certainly better than over the Channel.

It wasn't until just after midday that the squadron received the order to scramble. Twelve Spitfires, led by the CO, were airborne at 1215. Together with the Hurricanes of 607 Squadron, they patrolled the area between Beachy Head and Mayfield, north of Eastbourne, unaware that a major raid was crossing the Kent coast well to the east. It would eventually comprise 196 bombers, fighter-bombers and fighter escorts, with fighters outnumbering bombers 3:1.[73] All were bound for London.

Babbage landed after an uneventful hour-and-a-quarter, oblivious of the enormity of the occasion. There was a sense of business as usual as the CO headed off for lunch with the Tangmere station commander. Jack Boret was hosting the Under-Secretary of State for Air, Harold Balfour,[74] himself a decorated World War I flying ace. It meant that, unlike Babbage, Johnstone missed the next scramble: 12 more Spitfires at 1425. Patrolling further north this time, between Biggin Hill and Kenley, the squadron intercepted 15–20 Do 17s and Do 215s – part of the raid on London, now heading back to France. The lack of any top cover was surprising – probably due to the accompanying German fighters' limited endurance. The engagement that followed resulted in claims of three Do 17s and one Do 215 destroyed, plus a damaged Do 17 and Do 215. Given the loss of just a single Spitfire, it was a more than satisfactory return from the only encounter the squadron managed that momentous day.

Babbage's contribution to the action came when he singled out a Do 215 heading south, separated a mile or so to starboard of the rest of the enemy formation. Giving chase, he caught the bomber at 14,000ft somewhere near Beachy Head – it was hard to tell with cloud cover below. Setting up his Spitfire for a beam attack, a two-second burst closing from 250 to 100 yards saw his bullets strike home on the fuselage. He seemed to be getting the hang of this deflection shooting, but then suddenly he was too close! Forced to break off, up and away, he quickly repositioned directly astern for a second attack. A five-second burst, closing from 250 to around 80 yards saw the rear gunner's enclosure, at the back of the pilot's compartment, disappear in a shower of Perspex. Plainly he'd been killed – but not before return fire from his 7.92 machine guns had severely damaged Babbage's engine. While attacking from directly astern made life easier for an assailant, the same was true for a rear/tail gunner, of course.

As the bomber disappeared into cloud, Babbage realised that his protesting engine would never make it back to Westhampnett. But if he headed west for Shoreham, he might just be able to carry out a forced landing there. He really didn't fancy bailing out again, and anyway, aeroplanes were precious. With nothing to do now but set course in a gradual descent and wait, willing his trusty Merlin to keep going, he had time to reflect on just how fortunate he'd been. Had the Dornier gunner's rounds impacted just a few inches higher, his own cockpit would have been hit. There was something to be said for having the mass of a Rolls-Royce engine filling most of that forward fuselage. Needless to say, Babbage was more than a little relieved once he'd coaxed his damaged Spitfire safely back onto the ground. As an addendum to his latest narrow escape, his damaged Spitfire, X4412, was soon repaired and within a month was flying again, with 92 Squadron at Biggin Hill.

Landing more than 20 miles from Westhampnett meant that Babbage missed the final squadron scramble, late in the day. Little came of it though, confirming 602's minimal contribution to one of the most significant days in the RAF's history. The Luftwaffe's second major raid later in the afternoon saw 475 aircraft heading for London[75] – an armada said to have stretched for more than 70 miles across the sky. But again, its path was too far north, beyond the reach of 602's patrols.

At the end of the day, RAF claims stood at 185 German aircraft destroyed – the highest for a single day throughout the battle. Of these, 81 came in the morning and 104 in the afternoon. But as elsewhere, the reality was somewhat different: an adjusted total of 56 Luftwaffe losses against the RAF's 28. There's an interesting postscript to the associated aircrew losses: 12 pilots killed and 14 wounded.[76] Reflecting Park's intent to fight the battle overland, the RAF lost only one pilot offshore that day. Sergeant Jack Potter of 19 Squadron was shot down over the Channel. He bailed out of his Spitfire only to be picked up by a German He 59[77] and spend the rest of the war as a POW. But it was a lot better than drowning, as four out of every five who suffered a similar fate did that summer.

Transport was arranged to return Babbage to Westhampnett that evening, where he eventually completed his combat report to Henry Cranebrook's satisfaction. It was late before he got to bed but he was up first thing next morning – airborne before six with his flight commander, Findlay Boyd, for a 20-minute sortie. Less than two hours later he was airborne again when the squadron was scrambled for a longer patrol. All 12 aircraft flew for over an hour but saw nothing of the enemy. The day concluded with an evening patrol by a pair of aircraft, one of which was flown by the CO. It all seemed strangely quiet after the events of the previous day. While 602's involvement had been limited, it was clear to everyone, not least from excited radio reports the previous evening, that 15 September had been a pivotal day. The sense of anticlimax that Monday was almost palpable. But it ended in sadness when news came that Bill Coverley's body had been found by a tree on a farm near Tonbridge; he was still in his parachute, badly burned.

This strangely quiet period continued for the next three days. In part this was due to a deterioration in the weather; low cloud and rain had set in. But there was another more significant explanation. For a Luftwaffe told that the RAF was effectively on its knees, desperately short of aircraft, it was a severe blow to morale to find their two major raids of 15 September met by over 250 Spitfires and Hurricanes. The upshot was a variation in tactics that initially led to plenty of patrols – Babbage flew six times in two days – but apart from a brief skirmish on 17 September with a Ju 88 that disappeared into cloud, there was no contact with the Luftwaffe.

With only six sorties flown on 19 September, there was even time to visit the odd pub. The Ship at Bosham was a particular favourite, and it was there that evening that Sandy Johnstone dined with David Niven. One of the CO's companions (of whom more later) knew the actor, saw him sitting alone at another table and invited him to join them. Together with a reduction in the squadron's alert state, it brought a pleasant end to the quietest day since 602's move to the Sussex coast. On a similar occasion a few weeks later, Niven would reveal his patent frustration at being employed on public relations duties rather than in an operational role. Before becoming an actor, he'd enjoyed a brief post-Sandhurst army career. This, plus a sense of patriotism, led him to return from America and rejoin as a lieutenant early in the war – the only British actor to do so.

By now Babbage was acknowledged as one of the squadron's more accomplished pilots, both in terms of results and sheer piloting skill. He was flying as much as anyone; however, like his colleagues, there were few opportunities to add to his score. At this stage it stood at four confirmed enemy aircraft, one shared confirmed, one probable and one damaged. He was close to reaching the feted 'ace' status – five confirmed kills. And history would accord a particular status to those who earned this accolade during the Battle of Britain. That said, such thoughts were far from the mind of a quiet, reserved man who largely kept himself to himself. His chance would come, albeit not in the next few days – a period that culminated in a new squadron record: no operations whatsoever on 22 September.

By way of contrast, in the two previous days Babbage had seen plenty of flying, as had the squadron, but there was little to show for it. That said, 20 September was marked by a couple of interesting developments. First, he took part in a unique event. For the first time 602 Squadron was ordered to join with two other squadrons overhead Tangmere before patrolling over Mayfield to the north-east. Although Keith Park was no fan of the 'Big Wing' concept as espoused by AOC 12 Group, Air Vice-Marshal Trafford Leigh-Mallory[78] and his acolyte, Douglas Bader, OC 242 Squadron at Coltishall, he was more than happy to deploy large formations himself – provided they were properly controlled. Indeed, it was an approach the squadron would soon see repeated.

The second unique event, unrelated to the first, was the sighting of a large formation of Me 109s flying 'at a great height' above the squadron. Johnstone thought that they 'were possibly a batch of the new 109Es with modified engines giving them an advantage over us at height'. He would be proved right; it was a sensible decision to leave them alone. The latest Messerschmitts created new problems. Radar operators had trouble tracking these fast-moving, high-flying aircraft; the Observer Corps experienced similar difficulties. Moreover, pilots taking them on in unpressurised Spitfires at previously unheard-of altitudes soon began to feel the strain – physical demands that may possibly have had a bearing on unexplained incidents later in Babbage's career.

Next day was a busy one: 31 sorties and six scrambles. Babbage flew on two of them. A couple, including his first, were to provide cover for a convoy. His second, in the evening at 1800, was a patrol between Biggin Hill and Maidstone in combination with the Hurricanes of 213 Squadron. Three of the squadron's patrols brought engagements, resulting in the destruction of a Ju 88, damage to two more and a damaged Do 17. Confirmation of the first of these, claimed by Pilot Officers Lyall and Hanbury, lay in the wreckage near Bosham, where the aircraft crash-landed. While there was plenty of flying for Babbage, and plenty more yet to come, after the intensity of mid-August and the 15 September armadas, it was hard to avoid a sense that the worst had passed. Moreover, confidence was increasing that the threat of invasion had lifted – at least for now. Little did people know at the time that in the wake of the Luftwaffe's setbacks on 15 September, two days later Hitler issued an order deferring Operation Sealion indefinitely. Meanwhile, for 602 there was work still to be done.

Unusually for a month in which he flew so regularly, there was no flying for Babbage on 24 September. All he missed was a morning patrol where 602 accompanied the Hurricanes of 213 and 607 Squadrons, and an exciting moment later in the day for the latter. While patrolling with 602 over Portsmouth, 607's Hurricanes were attacked by naval gunfire and suffered considerable damage. All the accompanying Spitfires had to show for a day's efforts was a single damaged Me 110.[79] It was a similar story next day, when Babbage was back on the programme and flew twice: just a single damaged Me 110, found over Brighton. The level of flying effort required for such scant reward was becoming a matter of concern for the CO. In Johnstone's view, chalking up lots of hours with little to show for it was more exhausting for his crews than what he described as 'more active sorties, where one has the stimulus of battle to keep the adrenalin flowing'. Seeing pilots fall asleep in their chairs – on the floor even – he was becoming increasingly worried about the effects of accumulated tiredness. And well he might.

It dawned fine and sunny on the morning of 26 September but there was little activity for the pilots at Westhampnett, just a few two- and three-man patrols. Babbage flew mid-morning, just 30 minutes with Flying Officer Donald Jack. The action started later in the afternoon when the whole squadron, 12 aircraft, joined the Hurricanes of 213 and 607 Squadrons as the Tangmere Wing set off to intercept a raid heading for Southampton. The engagement that followed stretched from the coast to well beyond the Isle of Wight, with 602 claiming an Me 109, an Me 110 and two He 111s destroyed; in addition, two Me 109s and a He 111 were listed as probables. One of the bombers fell to Babbage's guns.

He took off as Green 2 but he and Green 3 soon became separated from their leader. In fact, the entire squadron seemed to have broken up as they manoeuvred to attack what appeared to be a disciplined, mutually protecting formation. He and his wingman burst through some 30–40 He 111s, firing hundreds of rounds at opportunity targets, albeit without any obvious return. There was still no sign of any fighter cover, so with plenty of targets to choose from, Babbage could now afford to be more selective. A climbing circuit out to sea left him well positioned to attack a southbound vic of three aircraft at 15,000ft. But it would be a difficult approach: a front quarter attack on the right-hand Heinkel. Opening fire at around 300 yards, he kept the firing button depressed for four seconds until he was dangerously close – too close in fact at 30 yards or so. Forced to break up and away sharply, he narrowly missed his mortally wounded prey. Turning to assess the results, he saw the bomber drop out of formation and spiral downwards. Better not follow it all the way down, he thought, lest the strangely absent enemy fighter cover should suddenly appear. Out of ammunition after firing 2,400 rounds, it was time to head home. But not before he had the satisfaction of seeing the Heinkel impact on the sea below.

Sergeant Cyril Babbage was a Battle of Britain ace – not that the thought crossed his mind until much later. His most recent brush with the Luftwaffe had been too close for comfort.

Next morning found him in the dispersal hut gazing out at distinctly unpromising weather. Not a great day for flying, he mused. He really didn't fancy an early sortie. But at 0850 he found himself one of ten aircraft scrambled, heading for Kent, where so much recent activity had been taking place. They set up a patrol initially over Mayfield at 15,000ft where they were joined by the Hurricanes of 213 Squadron. Just as they approached Dungeness, Babbage caught sight of some 30 Me 109s high above and immediately alerted his colleagues to the bounce. In the action that followed, Pilot Officer Douglas Gage was hit and his glycol tank damaged but he managed to crash land safely, without injury, at Bivelham Forge, Stonegate, near Mayfield. It was 602's only loss during an engagement where its pilots claimed a Ju 88, a He 111 and an Me 110, all destroyed.

The first of these again fell to Babbage, but not before he'd had a scare. He found himself singled out for special attention by three Me 109s. The only way to escape was to pull into a hard turn, nose down in a steep spiral to retain precious speed. Despite his aircraft sustaining minor damage, it seemed to do the trick. Once he recovered at sea level, there was no sign of his attackers. It was a feeling he'd experienced before in a skirmish: one moment the sky was filled with whirling aircraft and the next, total isolation. Well, not exactly. He latched onto a lone Ju 88 heading south at about 400ft. Checking first to see that he really had shaken off his pursuers, he set up for an attack from directly abeam. There was little to be gained by exposing himself to another rear gunner. He opened up at around 250 yards and continued firing until yet again he was perilously close to the bomber – barely 50 yards away when he broke off the attack. The well-armoured Ju 88 proved a difficult target and it took Babbage four more attacks and some 1,800 rounds before the German bomber finally crashed into the sea. The machine-gun damage his aircraft sustained early on, escaping the attention of the German fighters, turned out to be repairable on base; X4160 was back flying again four days later.

A sixth confirmed wasn't the only excitement for Babbage that day. His second sortie, a 12-aircraft scramble led by the CO, brought further results. Patrolling once again near Dungeness, it was a case of déjà vu: attacked by Me 109s – just two this time, again from above and again from behind. Once again he was saved by the Spitfire's performance. He turned hard into his attackers, forcing them to break away, whereupon one of them transferred his attention to a B Flight colleague, albeit with no obvious result. As the 109 broke off its attack Babbage was presented with a brief firing opportunity himself, head-on but slightly below the Luftwaffe fighter at about 15,000ft. Continuing to live dangerously, he had time for just a quick, two-second burst of 300 rounds, opening up at 250 yards and closing to 40 – would he never learn! But it was enough to see the Me 109 enter a 45-degree dive, belching thick black smoke. Sandy Johnstone, who saw it disappear, was happy to support the young sergeant's claim and declare the enemy aircraft 'probably destroyed'.

As it happened, the CO had only just returned from leave and was concerned by the nature of the damage inflicted on some of his aircraft the previous day: some 'nasty-looking shell-holes'. From this he deduced that his pilots had been attacking unescorted Ju 88s head-on – exposing themselves to the bombers' front guns. He could only hope that 'the lads are not becoming blasé and throwing caution to the wind'. Babbage's own experience was that in the mayhem of multiple aircraft engagements, fleeting opportunities for head-on attacks sometimes presented themselves. For the pilot who took them in preference to breaking away – potentially even more dangerous because it risked exposure to enemy guns – it became a case of 'kill or be killed'.

After such excitement, it was perhaps inevitable that the last three days of September proved something of an anti-climax for Babbage. He flew every day, but despite regular scrambles he saw no action. The only enemy engagement during this brief period came on the last day of the month. The CO led an attack on 12 Ju 88s heading north at 11,000ft near Bembridge on the Isle of Wight. In clear weather there was little opportunity for the bombers to escape the attention of 602's pilots. They claimed four destroyed, a probable and two damaged. One of the confirmed and a damaged went to Johnstone himself.

What followed later that day – were it not apocryphal – exemplifies the sense of unreality Babbage sometimes found it hard to escape. According to his memoir,[80] together with Virginia Gilliatt[81] the CO had been invited to dinner that evening with the Duke of Norfolk. But before he left for Arundel he had a prior appointment in the Tangmere guardroom. Arriving formally dressed he was surprised to find waiting for him there a young Luftwaffe officer, together with an interpreter, who'd requested to meet him. Imagine his surprise when Ju 88 pilot, Oberst Helmut Schwenhart, then presented the man who'd shot him down with his Luger, flying helmet, lifejacket and orange scarf – a good luck token from his mother that had plainly outlived its usefulness. Further research revealed that not only were there no survivors of the Ju 88 Johnstone shot down, no German POW of this name or rank was ever captured. This fabricated story remains in place, however, as an example of the perils, as well as the rewards of extensive research.

Despite being away for a week at the start of the month – the legacy of being shot down himself – September 1940 trumped August as Babbage's busiest month yet. He flew 30 operational sorties and 30 hours. It would be some time before he matched these figures, or indeed the quiet satisfaction of his achievements.

CHAPTER 7

END OF THE BATTLE

October would mark the end of the Battle of Britain; officially it concluded on the 31st. For Cyril Babbage and his colleagues, it would see a change in the nature of their activities. This was due mainly to the Luftwaffe's new modus operandi and exacerbated by the inhibiting autumn weather. With Dorniers and Heinkels now consigned almost exclusively to night bombing, and German raids focussed mainly on London, 602 Squadron's engagements became more sporadic. Of those that did occur, some were with Me 109s now operating in the fighter-bomber role, carrying a single 250kg bomb that brought performance penalties. It was therefore not unusual to see such aircraft jettison their external loads when attacked by RAF fighters.

A measure of this general reduction in operational intensity is that on only two days during the month did the Luftwaffe lose more than 20 aircraft; and on only six did Fighter Command lose ten or more. Looked at another way, the RAF was winning the numbers game 2:1. During the whole of October it lost 186 aircraft against a Luftwaffe figure of 379.[82] Aircraft could quickly be replaced – industry was outbuilding the Germans 2:1 in terms of single-engined fighters. And for every two new aircraft delivered to the front line, the civilian repair organisation was returning a third. The loss of 120 RAF pilots, however, was worrying and underlined the importance of Dowding's stabilisation scheme.

As if to emphasise the 'keep calm and carry on' spirit the government was keen to promote, life at Tangmere and Westhampnett reflected this stoical, business as usual attitude. Not that it greatly affected life for NCOs like Sergeant Cyril Babbage. His boss, on the other hand, continued to enjoy the company of the great and the good – David Niven, the Duke of Norfolk and the Duke of Hamilton, one of Johnstone's predecessors of whom more shortly. In fact, the first morning of the month was marked by a visit from the Duke of Norfolk. Such events were good for morale, as was the regular appearance of a YMCA mobile canteen manned by local volunteers. Some of these 'charming ladies' too were from the upper echelons of society, including the driving force, 25-year-old Virginia Gilliatt, the lady who first introduced the CO to David Niven. Dispensing libations with her on one such occasion was a woman once reputed to be the most beautiful in England, Lady Diana Duff Cooper.[83] It seemed that one way or another Johnstone and his auxiliaries, an eclectic team that included two Old Etonians, Pedro Hanbury and Mickey Mount, the latter an Oxford graduate, and a butcher's son in Cyril Babbage, held a certain fascination for the aristocracy. Glamour by association, perhaps.

No sooner had the duke's visit begun than the squadron was scrambled. He had the good grace to await the safe return of all 11 aircraft – and this despite one section being bounced by eight or ten Me 109s at 23,000ft over St Catherine's Point. Unusually in such circumstances, neither side inflicted any damage on the other.

Babbage missed this particular scramble but flew later that afternoon, together with three sorties next day, albeit the last two totalled only 15 minutes: two instantly recalled scrambles that did little for the nerves of those involved – five aircraft on the first occasion and the entire squadron, 12 Spitfires, on the second. The only claim that day was a Ju 88 destroyed ten miles off Selsey Bill by OC B Flight, Findlay Boyd; he was in company with Paddy Barthropp, to whom he conceded a miserly quarter share.

What followed was two days of poor weather, heavy rain and low cloud that allowed only a token three sorties on 4 October. Babbage managed three himself next day, a day of five scrambles, three involving the entire squadron – all to no avail. More heavy rain the following day limited flying to a single weather check. On 7 October, a day marked by a double tragedy, Babbage flew twice. The second occasion was when 602 was scrambled at 1530 to patrol the Southampton area together with 213 and 607 Squadrons. The 24 Hurricanes were flying below and slightly ahead of the Spitfires when the two 'weavers' providing cover at the rear crashed into one another. After they broke apart, a single parachute eventually appeared, leaving those who saw the accident with a sense of emptiness. It was such an unnecessary, avoidable loss.

As the patrol was about to head home, Flying Officer Jack and his No. 2, Sergeant Whall, were sent in pursuit of a solitary Do 17. First Jack and then Whall raked the bomber with accurate fire. There was no need for a second attack. It keeled over and crashed into the sea. As they turned for home, Whall joined on his leader's starboard side. Shortly after, and without a word, he peeled away and dived towards the ground. Jack was mystified and concerned. What accounted for Whall's failure to respond to any of his worried calls, and what could possibly have caused such unusual behaviour? He was sure that the Dornier hadn't opened fire on him, but that didn't rule out return fire in his No. 2's case. Perhaps he'd been hit. As a series of unanswered questions raced through his mind, all he could do was watch aghast as Whall flew straight into the ground near a farm at Lullington. There he was pulled from the wreckage and taken to the Princess Alice Hospital in nearby Eastbourne, only to die shortly after admission.

The cause of this tragedy would never be known but theories abounded. Sabotage was one; the after-effects of oxygen starvation another – they'd been patrolling at height. Or had he been hit by return fire? What about tiredness? Had Whall simply fallen asleep? Whatever the answer, it was hardly the sort of event to greet the arrival of the AOC. Air Vice-Marshal Keith Park had chosen an inauspicious day for a first visit to Tangmere's satellite in his personal Hurricane.

The very next day provided a stark reminder of just how serious could be the effects of exhaustion, both physical and mental. A Spitfire taxied erratically around the A Flight dispersal before finally shuddering to a halt. As the propeller flicked to a stop, ground crew ran towards the aircraft, where they could see the pilot slumped, head down in the cockpit. Had he been hit? There were no obvious signs of battle damage as they clambered up onto the port wing root to release him – only to find an individual best left unnamed snoring away peacefully!

The next few days were marked by more stormy weather – heavy rain and thick cloud cover that once again restricted flying operations. However, the conditions failed to deter a lone German raider. At 1900 on 8 October, half-an-hour after sunset, an unidentified aircraft overflew the airfield, machine guns blazing – thankfully to no effect. But it did lead to a change in the squadron's modus operandi. Henceforth two night-qualified pilots would remain on stand-by. Babbage didn't fit the bill; he hadn't flown at night since 27 June. He was therefore delighted to see the responsibility for what proved a fruitless exercise passed to Donald Jack and Andy McDowell. Another operational innovation introduced at the same time saw the squadron occasionally launch two- and three-man sections rather than all 12 aircraft. In part, though, this was also a response to continuing poor weather.

It wasn't just Westhampnett that was affected. The weather was so bad at Croydon next day that Archie McKellar, now a flight commander on 605 Squadron, diverted to Westhampnett together with a number of Hurricanes. Since leaving 602 he'd made a considerable name for himself, and just a couple of days later would be taking over his new squadron on promotion. By then he had 14 and three shared kills to his credit; moreover, 'full of enthusiasm', he boasted to Sandy Johnstone that two days earlier he'd shot down five Me 109s in a single day. Customary energy apart, Sandy Johnstone was taken aback by the change in this ebullient character; 'he looked very weary'. But this was hardly surprising, 'given the pressures under which the London-based squadrons are operating'. They were called upon more often than those at Tangmere and its satellite and seldom got 'a decent night's rest on account of the bombing'. The two friends' reunion may have been short-lived – Croydon's weather soon improved – but it left an indelible mark on Johnstone's psyche. It was the last time the pair would spend any time together. McKellar, 'certainly the bravest man' Johnstone ever met, would be

Above left: A young Cyril Babbage with mother, Beatrice. (Francis Wells)

Above right: Babbage with sisters Barbara and Betty. (Francis Wells)

Below: Ross Grammar School cricket team, July 1932. Babbage, in blazer, seated second right. (Herefordshire History)

Above: Babbage at stroke in a coxed four. (Babbage family archive)

Above: West Bank, the Babbage family home in Ross-on-Wye. (Francis Wells)

Below: A family gathering at West Bank. Seated left, Cyril's sisters Betty and Barbara. To the right: Cyril, centre, in front of (L-R) mother Beatrice, father Fred, Charlie and Gertrude Wells. (Francis Wells)

Above: A pre-war family outing. Back row (L-R): Babbage's father, Fred, and Cyril. Front row (L-R): sisters Betty and Barbara, Frank Wells and parents Gertrude and Charles. (Francis Wells)

Left: Sergeant Babbage during pilot training, 1939, before the award of his wings. (Francis Wells)

Below: The He 111 shot down by Squadron Leader Farquhar and Flying Officer Proudman, 602 Squadron, 9 February 1940. (Battle of Britain London Monument)

Top: HM King George VI meets Sergeant Babbage at Drem, 26 February 1940. (Francis Wells)

Above: No. 602 Squadron crews at readiness, Drem, early 1940. Babbage in the background with Flying Officer Archie McKellar lying down. Chess players: Flight Lieutenant Findlay Boyd (left) and Flying Officer Hector MacLean. (Francis Wells)

Left: Cuthbert Orde's sketch of John Peel, the beleaguered CO of 145 Squadron, the unit 602 Squadron replaced at Westhampnett.

Top: Grahame Algar's painting of Babbage being shot down by Hauptmann Mayer's Me 109, 26 August 1940. (Grahame Algar)

Above: Babbage clambers ashore at Bognor after his rescue. (Francis Wells)

Right: Babbage accepts the offer of a cigarette. (Francis Wells)

Left: Hauptmann Karl-Heinz Mayer. (Chris Goss)

Below: Known as Mayer-Ast, the man who shot Babbage down, with his Staffel, fourth from the right. (Chris Goss)

Bottom: Hauptmann Mayer in forage cap. Babbage was the 17th victory marked on his Me 109's tailfin. (Chris Goss)

Opposite page: The wreckage of Babbage's 602 Squadron Spitfire, X4541, after his forced landing near Iford Hill, 12 October 1940. (Francis Wells)

Left: Double Olympic champion Pilot Officer 'Billy' Fiske of 601 Squadron, Tangmere, the first American killed during the Battle of Britain. (Andy Saunders Collection)

Below: Pilot Officer Babbage with his first fiancée 'Mac' at Buckingham Palace for his investiture, 14 March 1941. (Babbage family archive)

Bottom: Pilot Officer 'Pedro' Hanbury, 602 Squadron. (Andy Saunders Collection)

killed just a few weeks later. Ironically, it was on the day after the Battle of Britain officially ended.

The event that probably had the greatest impact on Babbage as the battle drew towards its close was notification a day later, on 10 October, of the award of his DFM. It would not be gazetted until 25 October, when the citation would read, 'Sergeant Babbage has shown consistent keenness and ability in operations against the enemy. He has personally destroyed six enemy aircraft and probably one other.' Official recognition was no more than this self-contained and increasingly capable young man deserved. He'd earned it.

On a day marked by the award of a Bar to Findlay Boyd's DFC as well, there was news of a different kind too. Sergeant Sprague's body had finally been found, washed up on Brighton beach.

The following day saw the introduction of another innovation: an experimental dusk patrol. In company with his two night-qualified pilots, the CO took off in twilight at 1845. Aided by a waxing gibbous moon,[84] they patrolled as far east as Brighton. The intent was to cover Beachy Head, landfall for earlier German raids, in the hope of intercepting bombers en route to London. But it was not to be. Ground mist soon obscured the land, so Johnstone returned to Westhampnett, touching down with the assistance of the aircraft's landing light, while Jack and McDowell used the floodlights at Tangmere to recover safely.

12 October was also the day Babbage finally paid the penalty for continuing his attacks perilously close to the enemy. Together with Pilot Officers Fisher and Hart, he intercepted a Ju 88 at 10,000ft off Beachy Head. They shared a probable – but at a cost. After all three raked it with fire, the bomber limped away at 50ft on one engine with a badly damaged rudder – but not before its gunners had inflicted severe damage themselves. Thanks to bullets in the main spar, Hart's aircraft would require a new wing, while Babbage would be forced to crash land near Lewes with damage to his engine's glycol system. He touched down safely on a farm near Iford Hill, where he ran through a hedge before his wheels caught a small ditch which flipped his aircraft over onto its back. X4541was damaged beyond repair – another example of a Spitfire with a remarkably short service life: just six-and-a-half hours in the air.

Remarkably, Babbage escaped without major injury – just cuts and bruises. As with his earlier Bognor arrival, his experience produced a flood of photographs. One of them was clearly posed. It shows him wearing his trademark scarf, seated nonchalantly on the underside of the engine of his upturned aircraft. The giveaway is that he wasn't entitled to wear the DFM ribbon shown plainly on his tunic until a couple of weeks after his crash landing. Later on the day itself, he found himself being entertained by a couple in their nearby farmhouse, much to the delight of their young children. It brought an unusual end to his third and final sortie of the day – one he was more than thankful to survive. He'd finally paid the penalty for pressing home his attacks so aggressively.

There's one last addendum to this tale. Details of take-off and landing times, together with times of flight, are normally logged to the nearest five minutes. However, these three sorties appear in the squadron's ORB in uniquely precise fashion: take-off at 1517 for all three but landing for Babbage at 1536 and for his companions at 1555. It turns out to be a peculiarity repeated elsewhere in broadly similar circumstances – 'loss' of an aircraft.

Babbage didn't fly on operations again for a week, not that he missed much. Bad weather continued to limit the squadron's flying, and what patrols there were failed to find any enemy aircraft. Things were definitely quieter than before – on the south coast by day if not in London by night. Vere Hodgson, a charity worker living in Notting Hill, kept a wartime diary of her experiences.[85] It provides an eyewitness account of what it was like to live through the Blitz. On the day Babbage was shot down for the third time, she wrote, "They are here again. It is 8 p.m. How we are all going to escape I cannot imagine." Then two days later: "The devils are here now at 7 p.m. . . . we shall have to endure this until 6 a.m. The moon is full . . . so God help us." She continues, "What an awful night we had. They never ceased until after 5 a.m. We could not count the bombs we heard." On 16 October she wrote,

> "Well, in spite of it being the worst night of the blitzkrieg so far, I slept a few hours. From 11.30 to 1 a.m. Then I was awakened by frightful gunfire and numerous earth tremors. The house rocked like a cradle! So it went on all night."

Little wonder that the sympathies of 602 Squadron's pilots lay with the civilians who, frustratingly, they were all but powerless to defend.

The role of the controller at Tangmere, and at every sector station for that matter, was an important one. While all were trained in their responsibilities, they needed particular qualities. Relevant flying experience was important to their credibility – one of the reasons why George Pinkerton was at the time undergoing controller training at Stanmore – as was calmness under pressure and the ability to instil trust. A confident, reassuring voice to back up sound judgement helped enormously too. Managing the three squadrons at Tangmere and Westhampnett, plus a second satellite at Merston, used occasionally as a relief landing ground, could be a handful. Mistakes were made, albeit not with any regularity – witness September's night-flying debacle. There was another on 14 October which Babbage did well to avoid.

On his first day in the job, a new Tangmere controller launched 602 on a scramble in poor weather. The CO, who was at Tangmere at the time making arrangements for Sprague's funeral, was not best pleased when he learned of this. Before leaving Westhampnett he'd issued a grounding order after Mickey Mount, flying with Sergeant Smith early that morning, returned to announce that the weather simply wasn't fit for flying. By now, however, six aircraft from B Flight, including a couple of new and inexperienced pilots, were struggling after entering cloud at 500ft, shortly after take-off. There they remained, in the stygian greyness of solid cloud up to 25,000ft. An unimpressed Flight Lieutenant Donald Jack was fortunate to hold his flight together in such conditions. He heaved a metaphorical sigh of relief when they finally broke out into clearer weather. Alerted to the situation, Johnstone – no respecter of persons in this instance – was irate and immediately took control, guiding B Flight out to sea in a gentle descent. When Jack's formation eventually broke cloud at 800ft on their return to base they were finally able to relax. The tension in every cockpit had been hard to bear, the concentration intense. All six aircraft eventually landed safely at Westhampnett after an hour and 25 minutes of the most challenging flying any of them could remember – and that without a single sign of the Luftwaffe!

As the dust settled back at Tangmere, the senior controller, who'd arrived by now, was happy to exonerate OC 602's pre-emptive behaviour – not least because the scramble had been against the advice of others in the Tangmere ops room in the first place. An eventful day was rounded off by the arrival of Wing Commander the Duke of Hamilton, a previous OC 602 Squadron, for an overnight stay – one marked by an impromptu invitation to join the current CO for dinner at Arundel Castle once again.

Heavy rain and extensive cloud cover continued to impede operations as the month progressed. The squadron's first, fleeting contact with the Luftwaffe since Babbage's forced landing came eight days later: two quick bursts from Mickey Mount at a Ju 88 before it dived into cloud, apparently undamaged. He was back flying again by 22 October and regained night currency on his second sortie three days later – no fun in a Spitfire but a necessary evil. The intervening period brought a new weather hazard in the shape of the first fog of autumn. If the conditions put a damper on the squadron's activities, even more so did the loss of Babbage's B Flight colleague, 21-year-old Sergeant Dougie Elcome, on 26 October. They'd taken off together at 1210 but 35 minutes into a sortie that for the others would last little more than an hour, he peeled away from the formation, crashed and was killed. They were on patrol in the London area at 31,000ft when the incident occurred. One moment Elcome was in formation, the next he was gone, spiralling downwards effectively out of control. Shortly before impact he finally responded to the worried calls from his formation leader, but it was too late. All that followed his brief message was a hollow silence. Neither his body nor his aircraft has ever been found.

The remaining members of B Flight returned to Westhampnett in subdued fashion, mystified by their loss. The most likely explanation was hypoxia – oxygen starvation. Had Elcome's system failed? It would never be known. What was known is that in early September the young sergeant had been hospitalised for a period after being knocked unconscious when he crashed on Bognor golf course. He spent the next five weeks on the ground. Was there perhaps a connection between this enforced period of inactivity and his accident? Keen to return to flying, he did so on 14 October and thereafter enjoyed reasonable continuity, notwithstanding regular periods of bad weather. While no more is known of the latest of 602's unexplained losses, it's impossible not to draw comparisons with the earlier loss of Sergeant Whall, and the advent of high-flying Me 109Es.

The following day saw the squadron reopen their account when Sergeant McDowell claimed one Ju 88 destroyed plus another probable. But it represented only a limited return from an encounter with several enemy formations: initially 20–30 Ju 88s escorted by Me 109s and later a vic of five bombers that McDowell attacked. The only other pilot to engage was Pilot Officer Hopkins. Returning from a fruitless chase after a Me 109 he managed a quick but ineffective burst at another Ju 88. Babbage was destined to miss this welcome return to action. Frustratingly, he didn't fly on operations for the next two days, the second of which, 29 October, provided what was probably 602's most productive scramble thus far.

Led by Mickey Mount again, it was one of four flown that day and resulted in a classic encounter. Patrolling at 27,000ft, the squadron attacked two large formations of Me 109s below them at 23,000ft, roughly 30 in each and likely hampered by carrying bombs. Not only did the Spitfires of 602 have a significant height advantage, they also had the sun at their backs. The resulting claims were seven destroyed (one falling to Mount's guns), two probables and three damaged. Against this splendid haul, only one Spitfire incurred slight damage. And all this was achieved while the CO was on leave in Glasgow.

It was perhaps poetic justice that next day should see Babbage airborne again but on the other end of the stick, his formation bounced from high above by several Me 109s. In the resulting dogfight Pilot Officer Hanbury and Sergeant McDowell each destroyed an Me 109; two more were claimed as probables and another damaged. On the debit side, Sergeant Smith was wounded and crash-landed on the foreshore at Greatstone near Lydd; neither he nor his aircraft would ever fly again. Pilot Officer Douglas Gage was also forced down – for the second time. As on the previous occasion a month or so earlier, he crash-landed without injury, this time at Millbank Farm, Newchurch, near Lympne. Finally, Pilot Officer 'Pat' Lyall's aircraft also suffered light damage. Given their disadvantaged start, it was a creditable outcome from the squadron's perspective.

With no flying at all on 31 October, this brought to an end Cyril Babbage's contribution to the Battle of Britain. It comprised 113 sorties and more than

80 hours' operational flying, during which he accounted for six Luftwaffe aircraft destroyed (plus a share in a seventh), two probably destroyed (plus another shared) and two damaged. On the other side of the ledger, he survived being shot down three times but lost only two aircraft. It was a contribution of which he could be justifiably proud. A hardened veteran now, he'd certainly come a long way since those early days at Drem.

Babbage's achievements, and indeed those of his squadron, are all the more impressive when seen in perspective. When AOC 13 Group, 'Birdie' Saul, was required to identify replacement units to bolster 11 Group, he sensibly chose his most experienced squadrons. In bequeathing Keith Park the auxiliaries of 602 Squadron he was selecting a unit that had been tested since the earliest days of the war. Their performance would more than justify his decision. After coming late to a party that took place mainly in the skies over Kent, Surrey and Sussex, their claims of 102 aircraft destroyed during the battle were second only to the Poles of 303 Squadron who arrived even later, on 31 August. The latter's own score of 126,[86] even if exaggerated (which it was, by a factor of nearly three), bears testament to the abilities of a cohort of aggressive, experienced pilots determined to wreak revenge on their German oppressors. Having said this, later research[87] indicates that the Poles were only the third highest-scoring unit during the battle, behind both 603 and 609 Squadrons. By this reckoning 602 ranks equal seventh with 41 Squadron; but in terms of aircraft kill:loss ratios the squadron ranks third (at 2.4:1) after 609 (4.7:1) and 303 (2.8:1).

Statistics reinforce the value of the experience Park saw as so important. Towards the end of August, he gathered evidence to prove his point – evidence that reflects well on 602. In the short time since their arrival at Westhampnett, the squadron had claimed 26 Luftwaffe victims while incurring only two pilot casualties. Other units sent south by AOC 13 Group enjoyed similar levels of initial success: 41 Squadron, with whom Babbage would later serve, claimed 13 kills for only a single pilot casualty.[88] These figures are even more significant when seen in the light of changing circumstances. The early days of the battle saw the Luftwaffe deploy relatively large numbers of comparatively vulnerable aircraft like the Ju 87, but by late August this was a thing of the past. The ratio of fighters to bombers was increasing as well, to as much as 5:1, making it increasingly difficult to get through to Park's primary targets, the bombers capable of creating havoc on the ground.

On the other side of this coin are the losses suffered by inexperienced units joining the main battle for the first time. In late August, shortly after arriving at Biggin Hill, 79 Squadron lost four aircraft together with their pilots on the same day. For 603 and 222 at Hornchurch the figures were equally worrying: three aircraft and their pilots for the former, six and three pilots for the latter – both in a single day.[89] These sorts of results, little short of devastating, were plainly unsustainable. They can probably be put down to inexperience, although 603 Squadron's performance plainly improved rapidly. In any event, such losses supported the introduction of Dowding's stabilisation scheme. The Luftwaffe on the other hand had learned from its experience in another guise during the Spanish Civil War and applied these lessons in the invasion of Poland and subjugation of France that followed. All of which put a premium on the RAF's experienced pilots, a dwindling resource as the battle continued. That said, the Luftwaffe was also losing battle-hardened crews at a worrying rate.

In addition to their experienced CO, 602 Squadron produced three more Battle of Britain aces. That Babbage should now find himself in such company is little short of remarkable. Amongst the 3,000 or so who comprised Churchill's fabled 'Few', only limited numbers earned this accolade, let alone NCOs as young and inexperienced. Just 23, he was in the early stages of a flying career that would continue for many a year yet. What's more, Babbage's achievements brook no argument. His first five confirmed victories were credited to him and him alone. As time wore on, the ace moniker came to be used more loosely and was applied also to those whose victories included partial claims – a third here, a half there. That Babbage's five were achieved unaided adds further to his burgeoning reputation.

CHAPTER 8

THE WAR GOES ON

THE BATTLE OF BRITAIN MAY have been over, at least officially, but the war went on. As October became November, the weather that governed flying operations took a distinct turn for the worse. More heavy rain meant that Westhampnett became a quagmire in places. That said, Babbage flew every day of the first week – bar 3 November, when not a wheel, far less a propeller, was turned – but to little tangible effect. If the Luftwaffe hadn't lost interest, there was certainly a reduction in their efforts. It wasn't until 6 November that the squadron encountered any enemy aircraft. An engagement that afternoon with an unusually ragged Me 109 formation (they'd possibly been attacked previously) at 26,000ft near Portsmouth brought its rewards, albeit none for Babbage. The squadron claimed one Me 109 plus a shared destroyed and two more shared damaged. In a separate action later that day, a shared Ju 88 would be added to the tally. As if by way of retribution, that night 602's base was again attacked by a lone aircraft: a Ju 88 that delivered a stick of incendiaries that fortunately did little damage.

The event of the month, if not the year, came on the evening of Thursday 7 November: a major party in the Tangmere officers' mess that exemplified the sense of dislocation, of separation from reality, that Babbage sometimes felt. It was the brainchild of the station commander. On the pretext that should the Germans invade, there would be nothing left in mess funds for them to enjoy, Jack Boret ordered the committee to organise a 'super function'. They did him proud. Even Dowding put in a brief appearance at a spectacular party where guests ranged from the Crazy Gang,[90] whose Bud Flanagan was pressed into service as an auxiliary barman, and showgirls from the Windmill theatre (monopolised by Flanagan's colleagues) to ministers of the crown, including Harold Balfour, and even the government chief whip.

It's a matter of conjecture whether Babbage and his ilk were invited to what was by all accounts a memorable event. It seems unlikely. Had they been, would they have been keen to attend? In one sense – squadron unity – the answer is probably, yes. In another – the preponderance of senior officers and the extensive guest list – it's probably, no. NCOs, airmen too for that matter, had their own social circles. Moreover, Babbage himself was more than content with his own company. Where the mixing of officers and other ranks occurred outside the working environment it tended to be at events arranged for just such a purpose, e.g. beer calls or parties to celebrate a significant occasion or event. Not that there was much scope for such activities in wartime. But these questions raise a wider issue: the incongruity of social separation between officers and NCOs when their waking hours were spent cheek by jowl in dispersal huts. And when individual survival day-to-day depended on the closest possible professional integration between squadron members, regardless of rank. In these close-knit communities it wasn't unusual for the niceties of rank to be conveniently forgotten and replaced by nicknames, or even first names – and without any loss of respect. It's an issue to which we will return.

Babbage flew regularly when the November weather allowed, but he was frustrated on two counts. First, he missed the only action in the first half of the month. On 8 November, the day Mickey Mount's DFC was announced, a patrol found a Ju 88 near Selsey Bill and inflicted a degree of damage as it raced back across the Channel. Five days later another patrol deposited a Ju 88 into the sea near Brighton, albeit with Hurricane assistance. Babbage's second frustration came from finally succumbing to the flu bug that had been ravaging the squadron, denuding 602 of pilots. He was grounded for ten days but didn't miss much. And there was little to excite once he returned to flying on 26 November: few patrols and minimal enemy engagements. As Sandy Johnstone put it: "The Germans have definitely lifted the pressure and we are now under no more strain than we were during our service in Scotland."

As this quiet, anticlimactic month drew to a close, Babbage lost a friend and colleague, Pilot Officer Pat Lyall, in tragic and unusual circumstances – circumstances that had more than a hint of déjà vu about them. It was on 28 November, the day that Dowding's successor, Air Chief Marshal Sir Sholto Douglas,[91] chose to visit the squadron. To his credit, this was only four days after he'd taken over Fighter Command from a man history would treat more kindly than did his own service at the time.[92] Inevitably, there was a scramble. Enemy aircraft had been detected crossing the Channel, heading for the Isle of Wight. With the CO engaged elsewhere, Mickey Mount took the lead. Unusually, he was tasked with patrolling at 33,000ft – a height where the Spitfire was no match for the gaggle of Me 109Es which bounced them from above. After a fierce battle in difficult circumstances, they got away lightly; Lyall's was the only aircraft to be hit. The extent of the damage wasn't clear, but he appeared to be making for a safe landing on the Isle of Wight. Then suddenly, at about 1,000ft, he bailed out. With no time for his parachute to open, he was killed instantly when he hit the ground near Shanklin. It was a sad and curious incident.[93]

When the three Tangmere sector squadron commanders were called to discuss this latest debacle with Jack Boret they were livid. Sending 602 to patrol at an altitude which left their Spitfires vulnerable had cost a pilot his life. With the benefit of hindsight, Boret mused that the situation might have been avoided had Mount refused to accept the assigned altitude. That said, he acknowledged that blame couldn't be laid at the formation leader's feet. It lay squarely with the controller. He was called in and quickly reduced to tears by the sector commander's invective. But tears wouldn't bring back a lost colleague.

The bad weather on 8 December that continued to put a damper on operations meant that there was a good attendance at Pat Lyall's funeral in Brighton. This meant a lot to his mother, who'd requested a local ceremony rather than one in Scotland simply so that his colleagues could attend. When the CO returned to the squadron, he had happier news to impart: a commission had been announced. The Form 1406, Confidential 'R.A.F. Officers Record of Service', for Pilot Officer Cyril Frederick Babbage DFM would show his new service number, 89298, and note in the 'Movements' section his initial posting, to 602 Squadron on that very day. As if to confirm his change of status, the ORB records a single sortie the following day for Pilot Officer Babbage, who then disappears from sight, flying not a single operation for three weeks or so.

As the squadron's newest commissioned officer departed on a period of well-deserved leave, there was an end of term as well as an end of year feel about Westhampnett. The final scramble of the year, on 11 December, an encounter with several Me 109s, saw Pilot Officer Jake Edy, shot down. Wounded, and with a large part of one wing missing, the Canadian managed to crash land in a field near Folkestone. But his aircraft was a write-off. It effectively brought an untypical and less than memorable end to the squadron's stay at Westhampnett. Things were about to change.

Next day came news that the squadron was to return to Scotland, to Prestwick; they would be replaced by 610 Squadron from Acklington. The auxiliaries of 602 had proved their worth in the war 'down south', but Sandy Johnstone would be returning whence he came with a very different cohort. The original Scots representation, so important to a unit known as 'Glasgow's own' and exemplified by the likes of Archie McKellar, had been more than a little diluted. Postings in and out, notably that of another of the squadron's aces, Findlay Boyd,[94] on promotion to command 54 Squadron, meant that stalwarts like Babbage apart, the man who would remain in command could barely recognise his new team. How would they take the move – and indeed the change in operational tempo?

There was still time to recognise the achievements of another of 602's original members. Ten days after the award of a Bar to his DFM, Sergeant Andy McDowell[95] learned that he too had been awarded a commission. The last mentioned of the squadron's Battle of Britain aces and the most successful, it would be April 1945 before he added further to his tally. OC 616 Squadron at the time and flying a Meteor, he destroyed a Ju 88 on the ground. It was a fitting epitaph to the operational career of an exceptional pilot, one who exemplified the spirit and aggression that led Babbage and his colleagues to contribute so much to the RAF's famous victory in the summer of 1940.

CHAPTER 9

NEW BEGINNINGS

DRESSED IN HIS NEW OFFICER'S uniform, but still wearing his customary spotted scarf, Babbage arrived at Prestwick on 4 January 1941 in a Spitfire he'd been sent to pick up from Tangmere. It was one of a pair, the other flown by Nigel Rose, delayed by the same bad weather that would be a feature of the next few months. They arrived at the squadron bearing the good news that they'd both become engaged. The bad news was that operating now from Scotland, the pair would suffer the same frustrations that afflicted all loved ones separated in time of war. While his colleague solved the problem by marrying three months later, Babbage's own relationship didn't last; it eventually fell victim to these very circumstances.

In a way, his posting was unusual. He'd already completed a year's unbroken service on a front-line squadron and could reasonably have expected something different, an OTU posting perhaps, like some of his colleagues. That said, his position was far from unique. After even lengthier periods on operations, and under far more pressure than he was, both his current squadron commander and previous flight commander were continuing in command appointments. On balance, he felt that a return to the relative quiet of 13 Group could have been worse. Importantly, he was still doing the thing that he loved: flying Spitfires.

The new year at Prestwick was marked by tragedy, the death of Amy Johnson in a flying accident. On 5 January 1941 she bailed out over the Thames estuary when the Oxford she was delivering for the Air Transport Auxiliary ran out of fuel. Missing, believed drowned, her body was never found. The loss of this pioneering aviatrix, who'd spent the previous week or so marooned at Prestwick by bad weather, was deeply felt on 602 Squadron. The CO, who was staying in the same Glasgow hotel, had invited her to their New Year's Eve party where she made quite an impression on all those she met. The young pilots in particular were captivated by her personality as much as by her flying stories. Even for battle-hardened aircrew accustomed to tragedy and bereavement, hers seemed a particularly sad and unnecessary loss.

But life moved on, and Babbage's first month back in Scotland set the pattern for what was to come. Thanks mainly to unhelpful weather, fog in particular, he flew only six operational sorties in January – heaving a sigh of relief too after completing his first night patrol since late October. It was an experience he'd repeat as night patrols became a regular feature of the flying programme. Reflecting the lack of operational activity, albeit there was plenty of practice flying, for the fortnight from 26 January to 8 February he was detached to 58 OTU at Grangemouth. Formed just a few weeks earlier, in December 1940, the unit was short of experienced pilots to train those converting to the Spitfire. Lack of experience was becoming a factor on 602 Squadron too. Not long after Babbage's return, on 16 February the newly arrived Sergeant Booty ran into a Tiger Moth on landing. His Spitfire emerged undamaged, however, which is more than could be said for the aircraft he hit.

With a blitz on Glasgow anticipated shortly, experienced pilots, especially night operational crews, were now at a premium. But when the Clydeside raids eventually arrived, on the nights of 13 and 14 March, there was little the RAF could do, particularly on the second night when low mist grounded the squadron. And Babbage himself could do nothing; he was away on duty. On the morning of 14 March he was attending an investiture at Buckingham Palace where he received his DFM from HM King George VI.

Despite careful planning and rehearsal, locating let alone bringing down the Luftwaffe bombers proved all but impossible. Guided by their *Knickebein* radio-navigation system, they found their marks: an armament factory, a shipyard and an engine works. Official records show that 528 civilians were killed and 617 seriously injured.[96] After taking part in the squadron's futile efforts on the first night – seven sorties flown by just four pilots – and with telephone lines down, an anxious Sandy Johnstone drove to Glasgow to check that his wife was safe. Despite evidence of destruction all around, he was amazed to find their home almost untouched; the only damage was a broken kitchen window. In light of what followed, his decision to return the heavily pregnant Mrs Johnstone to the Orangefield Hotel, Prestwick's unofficial officers' mess, was a wise one.

Notwithstanding the emphasis on night flying, operational sorties became increasingly rare as the year wore on: just the odd convoy patrol and one or two 'flaps' – scrambles against unidentified targets. Some turned out to be 'friendlies', others simply disappeared. During the limited flying that was possible before the weather began to improve, the emphasis was on bringing the squadron's new arrivals up to speed. And there were lots of them. But how things had changed! Babbage couldn't help casting his mind back a year or so to when he was in a similar position himself, albeit then he didn't have the prior Spitfire experience these youngsters boasted now – not that it was proof against the occasional unfortunate episode.

For his remaining months on the squadron – he was destined to depart in June – it was very much the same story. There was plenty of practice flying but Babbage never flew more than a handful of uneventful operational sorties in any month, even after the weather finally began to improve. For the reducing number of Westhampnett veterans, the occasional sense of a disconnect from reality was magnified by any number of extraneous events: civic invitations, press visits, the CO's emergence as a radio personality (through a BBC talk on his Battle of Britain experiences), film crews from 20th Century Fox shooting footage for *A Yank in the RAF* that would be used repeatedly thereafter,[97] and regular visits from the great and the good. Foremost amongst the latter were the King and Queen. Theirs was combined with a visit to Glasgow, some 30 miles away, where members of the squadron were involved in associated events.

Meanwhile at Prestwick the squadron played host to more royalty in the shape of the Duke of Kent. Other visitors included various members of the RAF's upper echelons: the newly appointed AOC 13 Group, Air Vice-Marshal Jock Andrews,[98] and Lord Trenchard[99] himself. After refusing several of the prime minister's mooted appointments in support of the war effort, the 'father of the RAF' had taken upon himself an unofficial role as the service's Inspector-General. Then, less than two weeks after Trenchard's visit, the RAF's official Inspector-General,[100] arrived on a similar mission.

As time wore on, life settled into the same pattern that Babbage remembered from his previous Scottish incarnation: a relocation or two, regular incidents and a few accidents. As the culmination of a badly managed move in mid-April to the old racecourse at Ayr, two of the first aircraft to arrive crashed, one due to engine failure, the other with undercarriage problems. Then the brief detachment to Montrose that followed was marked by bent propellers and more undercarriage failures.

Coincident with the Ayr relocation came Sandy Johnstone's posting to controller duties at Turnhouse on 14 April. If life for his replacement, Squadron Leader John Kilmartin,[101] began inauspiciously, it soon got worse. He'd been in post less than a fortnight when, on 25 April, Sergeant Nicholson went missing barely three days after his arrival from Hawarden; it would be a further ten days before his body was picked up from the Irish Sea. Then in late May, less than three weeks after his fleeting night success – possible damage to an unidentified enemy bomber – Sergeant W.L. Brown[102] was killed in a mid-air collision practising 'synchronised dive attacks'; the other Spitfire recovered safely, albeit damaged. Added to the Blenheim, Beaufort and Beaufighter fatalities either on or near the airfield that marked his time back in Scotland, Babbage felt he'd seen more than enough of aircraft losses.

These sad developments tended to obscure the squadron's near brush with history. On 10 May a newly arrived flight commander, New Zealander Flight Lieutenant Al Deere,[103] was in one of two aircraft launched on an abortive mission. The Me 110 they were scrambled to intercept crashed after its pilot bailed out. Hitler's deputy, Rudolf Hess, apparently on a peace mission, had run out of fuel just south of Glasgow. Deere himself would go on to take part in the merry-go-round of 602 Squadron COs that would follow shortly.

After the stability of the Johnstone era, Kilmartin would remain in post for just seven weeks – moved on to a supernumerary position, assisting with the formation of the RAF's third Czech fighter unit, 313 Squadron. His replacement, Squadron Leader Patrick Meagher,[104] took over on 4 June, to be greeted almost immediately by a depressingly familiar event. Six days later, fresh from 57 OTU at Hawarden and flying his first squadron sortie, Sergeant O'Connor overturned on landing. After his Spitfire ended up on its back, he was immediately 'confined to bed in station sick quarters suffering from shock'. Then Babbage himself was posted: to 41 Squadron at Catterick on 12 June. He was ready to move on – as would Meagher, destined to prove another short-term incumbent; he would hand over to Al Deere on 1 August.

Looking back on his second stay in Scotland, in some ways Babbage found it a strange experience, exemplified by a number of unrelated memories. First, for a man who like most aircrew hated to see loose ends, there were the unsolved mysteries. Two building fires within days of each other early in his time at Prestwick defied explanation. Not long after came the worrying discovery of two sticks of gelignite wedged into the fuel system of the aircraft Ginger Whall had crash-landed near Bognor on 18 August 1940. Found when the wreckage of L1019 was recovered from Elmer Sands and dismantled, they inevitably raised questions over his subsequent demise – that of others too. Could it possibly have been attempted sabotage? Finally, there were a couple of events in March that illustrated the disconnect with reality that occasionally troubled Babbage. Like most of his junior colleagues, he was unaccustomed to the generous hospitality provided by the new station commander at Ayr, Wing Commander Loel Guinness,[105] who entertained the squadron's officers to supper in the house he'd rented near Troon. As the ORB succinctly put it, 'Very nice too!' This followed just a day after the Lord Provost of Glasgow[106] had provided three officers and about 20 'troops' with a similarly generous lunch; 'A good time was had by all!'

Enough of looking back, though. It was time to look forward. As he packed his bags for the journey south, what, he wondered, did the future hold for Pilot Officer C.F. Babbage DFM?

CHAPTER 10

A CHANGE OF SCENE

When Babbage arrived at Catterick, a sector station near Middlesborough in Yorkshire, his new unit was enjoying a rest and re-equipment period. After nearly six taxing months, 41 Squadron's move to the relative quiet of 13 Group on 23 February 1941 was an acknowledgement of the mauling it had suffered. Of the 18 pilots who arrived at Hornchurch on 3 September 1940, only four remained. These statistics hide a darker story. During this period 16 were killed, five so badly wounded they would never return to flying and another 15 posted away. A further measure of the squadron's travails is that the current CO, Squadron Leader Donald Finlay,[107] was 41's fourth boss in ten months. What lay behind this rapid turnover?

The story began with the events of 5 September 1940. Two major German raids comprising hundreds of aircraft and centred on London and Kent, provided 41 Squadron with arguably its most difficult test. As a result of the intense air activity that day, seven pilots – roughly a third of the squadron – came to grief in one way or another. Amongst those killed was the CO, Squadron Leader 'Robin' Hood,[108] who'd been in command since 22 April. Shot down over Essex, his aircraft broke up and his body was never found.

It was three days before his replacement arrived; however, Squadron Leader Robert Lister[109] lasted less than a week. Shot down on 14 September, his wounds were serious enough for him to be replaced that same evening. Squadron Leader Don Finlay thus became 41's third CO in ten days. Aloof, reserved and a strict disciplinarian, his prior claim to fame was as an athlete. Third in the Olympic 110 metres (120 yards as it was then) hurdles final in Los Angeles, he improved to second place in Paris four years later.[110] Babbage was about to come under the watchful eye of a unique individual, certainly in RAF terms – but only for a short time. Finlay would relinquish command in less than two months, by which time a good deal would have changed.

For the present, the squadron was spared the rigours of regular engagement with an enemy whose own tempo had slowed in similar fashion. The Blitz finally ended on the night of 10/11 May 1941, a month before Babbage arrived, although sporadic raids would continue, some of them substantial. The upshot for 41 was limited operational tasking and regular patrols, many of them at night. It all added up to minimal contact with the Luftwaffe. Babbage would fly just three operational sorties during what was left of June, a period spent familiarising himself with his new environment, flying practice sorties and regaining night currency.

There was a familiar feel about his introduction to his new squadron. In the early morning of his second day, 13 June, Pilot Officer Nigel Keable ran out of runway landing at nearby Thornaby after a practice sortie. He continued onto rough ground where his Spitfire was damaged when it tipped onto its nose. He could offer no excuse and was found entirely to blame. That said, with barely 180 hours in his logbook, 100 or so on the Spitfire, the 21-year-old was hardly a seasoned campaigner, although he had suffered a previous accident that wasn't his fault. A month after joining the squadron, landing after a non-operational night sortie on 14 April, he clipped the control hut and lost a wheel. His subsequent one-wheel landing was blamed on a faulty runway glide-angle indicator. The accident form (A.M. Form 1180) shows that at the time he had logged 118 flying hours, with just 51 on Spitfires, thus revealing an inconsistency. It suggests that in the two months between these two incidents he flew 62 hours total, 49 on the Spitfire – intensive flying figures at odds with the ORB. While subsequent accident-related flying hours must therefore be seen as suspect, they nevertheless give a feel for the general levels of experience on 41 Squadron.

Babbage flew his first night patrol with Keable on 25 June, a 55-minute sortie. It would prove Keable's last at Catterick. He was posted to 603 Squadron next day, having been with 41 barely three months. Seven weeks later, on 5 August, he would fall victim to Leutnant Erich Rudorffer.[111] The German ace figures later in the annals of 41 Squadron. For now, suffice it to say that Keable was shot down and killed over the North Sea during a circus[112] operation, escorting Blenheims as they bombed targets near St Omer.

While a squadron's assigned role in a circus varied, e.g. escort, target support, diversion, each operation amounted to the same thing: a squadron strength offensive sweep designed to engage enemy fighters. Babbage missed the single such operation 41 Squadron flew later that month, an 11 Group circus on 27 June. He could only watch enviously as 12 pilots took off for Redhill, a Kenley satellite, and a rare piece of excitement – the sort of mission that would soon form his staple diet. On this occasion 24 Blenheims set off to bomb engineering works near Lille, escorted by 19 fighter squadrons from 11, 12 and 13 Groups. It mattered not that 41's role in Circus 25 was a relatively minor one, rear diversion support, it provided those who took part with a tantalising foretaste of what was to come.

Returning to the familiar theme that greeted his arrival, two days before Babbage flew his first operational sortie, an uneventful 50-minute patrol with a fellow new arrival, Sergeant 'Cloudy' Rayner on 19 June, there was another accident. Sergeant Herbert Thorne crashed on landing at Leeming after a practice sortie; fortunately, the damage was repairable. The airfield was unfamiliar to him and once again inexperience played its part. Of just over 120 hours in Thorne's logbook, less than half were on Spitfires. In early July, after barely a month on the squadron, Thorne would find himself posted – to Babbage's old squadron as it happened. Three days later, on 22 June, came a similar story. Another new pilot, Australian Sergeant Alan Bull, seeking to secure his night operational status two weeks after joining, burst a tyre on landing; it caught the edge of the runway, causing his undercarriage to collapse. With a similar background to Thorne, around 150 hours with roughly a third on Spitfires,[113] the perils of night flying simply exacerbated the problems stemming from lack of experience. In the same way that Babbage learned from Archie McKellar, he would now become responsible for bringing on the young tyro. The process began six days later when he flew a 15-minute late-evening patrol in company with Bull.

To conclude the catalogue of errors that coincided with the new man's first couple of weeks at Catterick, on 26 June Sergeant Harold Fowler overshot the runway at Greatham, a satellite airfield, and skidded into a blister (portable) hangar. It was a similar story: 184 flying hours, 90 on the Spitfire. He was posted immediately to 13 Group's Anti-Aircraft Cooperation Unit at Turnhouse. To Babbage, Catterick began to feel like Drem revisited – a sense prompted earlier by the arrival of a familiar face, the AOC, Air Vice-Marshal Jock Andrews, for a station visit on 21 June. This time he had in tow the Secretary of State for Air, Sir Archibald Sinclair.

As June became July it was more of the same: little operational flying but, mercifully, fewer accidents – at least in the early days. With the odd raid appearing on the radar plot, and disappearing almost as quickly, standing patrols were the order of the day – nights too. After an uneventful 45 minutes patrolling overhead base in the early afternoon of 6 July, again with Sergeant Bull, Babbage flew two brief night patrols on 8 July, 15 and 30 minutes respectively. Earlier in the day, the accident-prone sergeant had survived another landing incident. This time, though, he was absolved of any blame. The pile of rubbish that caused his undercarriage to collapse at Greatham was all but invisible in the long grass – grass that should have been cut!

Next day Babbage had his first inkling of a problem to which there seemed no obvious solution: the rapid turnover of personnel. As an experienced pilot he now felt reasonably secure, but he found it difficult to understand some of the squadron movements. Sergeant William Menzies was a prime example. Posted in on the first of the month, on 8 July he was on his way again: to 123 Squadron at Turnhouse before he'd flown a single operational sortie. Babbage could only wonder at the logic behind this – unless, of course, it was to make room for the experience that was at a premium on his own squadron.

Tangible reward for 41's patrol efforts finally came on the night of 11 July (or rather the early hours of 12 July) when Pilot Officer Geoffrey Ranger brought down a He 111. His achievement illustrates just how dangerous such activity could be, and how difficult it was to secure a night kill. Ranger was one of six pilots airborne at 0135 (a seventh followed shortly after), ordered to patrol ten miles north and south of Whitby at heights up to 17,000ft, separated at 1,000ft intervals. He caught sight of an aircraft briefly illuminated by searchlight, 1,000ft below him at 8,000ft. Aided in part by waning moonlight (it was 16 days since full moon), he set up for a stern attack: a four-second burst from 350 down to 50 yards. It was difficult to assess closing speeds in such conditions and he soon found himself far too close. Forced to break upwards and away, he kept sight of his quarry thanks mainly to an amber light on the tail that remained illuminated throughout. Three further attacks followed, quarter to astern, each one similar: four seconds of fire, closing from 350 down to 100 yards. Out of ammunition, Ranger followed the Heinkel down until it disappeared into a haze at 4,000ft. Unable to see the results of his attacks because of tracer fire from the Heinkel's dorsal gunner, he was gratified to learn that the bomber eventually ditched off Flamborough Head. In return for the 2,703 rounds he fired (17 remained in a jammed machine gun), his aircraft took a single German bullet, lodged in the starboard main spar.

Dawn brought poor weather. With no operational flying, limited practice was the order of the day. It came as little surprise to Babbage that the unfortunate Alan Bull experienced another incident on landing, although once again no blame was attached. His burst tyre was attributed to a ridge by the Catterick runway. Similar problems were the cause of a parallel incident on 14 July when Sergeant Leonard Hunt's first sortie ended with a collapsed undercarriage. There was a pattern here. That said, it was Hunt's first sortie in a Spitfire, and he had an excuse. He lost control when his aircraft bounced after he hit the 'exposed and protruding' runway lip on landing – a problem caused by subsidence. Once again, no blame was attached.

As the month progressed, Babbage's operational flying was limited to convoy support and standing patrols – three relatively short sorties of less than an hour. Like many of his colleagues, he was bored by the sameness of their Catterick existence. The Luftwaffe seemed to have drawn in its offensive horns. Unfortunately, this sameness continued in the shape of regular incidents and accidents. On 22 July another new arrival, Sergeant

Denys Smallbone, careered off the end of the runway and buried his aircraft in a gun emplacement. It's a measure of the RAF's need for front-line pilots that this particular individual had only 113 hours total, 46 on the Spitfire. Six days later he was posted to 43 Squadron at Drem, flying Hurricanes; he'd spent just two weeks with the squadron. If Smallbone's figures are to be believed,[114] even Battle of Britain neophytes were more experienced. While Geoffrey Wellum had no Spitfire time when he joined 92 Squadron, he did have 168 hours total – and that was without finally completing his training.

Then on 24 July Pilot Officer Ranger contrived to collapse his undercarriage after bursting a tyre at Hucknall landing after a practice sortie. However, he was absolved of any blame because the rough ground where he touched down was deemed dangerous. His experience was typical of those involved in such incidents: 189 flying hours with 69 on the Spitfire.

28 July marked the change that Babbage and his colleagues had been hoping for: relocation to Merston, a Tangmere satellite, and a move from defensive to offensive operations. In the wider context this was a response to Operation Barbarossa, the invasion of the Soviet Union a few weeks earlier that saw German troops moved to a second front and a parallel reduction in the Luftwaffe's night raids. Babbage's initial role in the move would be less than exciting: officer i/c the rail party, comprising 117 NCOs and airmen. But there was still time to record the odd notable event. He and Alan Bull had earlier flown the last two operational sorties in the squadron's Mk II Spitfires, an uneventful 35-minute convoy patrol on 25 July. To complete this set of aircraft statistics, a day earlier Pilot Officer Marx 'Mark' Williams had claimed the squadron's final Mk II success – a damaged Ju 88 some 50 miles off Teesmouth. His aircraft also became the last Mk II casualty when a bullet was found lodged in his tailplane.

On 28 July 1941, Pilot Officer Babbage's final official duty at Catterick was to attend a parade and roll call at 0630, after which his party marched to Catterick Bridge railway station. The next, exciting phase of his career was about to begin.

CHAPTER 11

THE BEST FORM OF DEFENCE

RETURNING TO THE TANGMERE SECTOR felt like a homecoming for Babbage. It seemed only weeks ago that he was last here; in reality it was eight months since he had left Westhampnett. That said, the squadron's new home, Merston, was unfamiliar. Barely three miles south of Tangmere, with Westhampnett a similar distance to the north-west forming a triangle, it had been in operation only since May. Set up originally as a dummy airfield to draw Luftwaffe attacks away from main operating bases, its fake buildings were replaced by the real thing as Tangmere's importance increased. By the time 41 Squadron arrived it was reasonably well found: permanent buildings, blister hangars and even fighter pens.

In operational terms, 41 would come under the direct command of Tangmere's Wing Commander Flying, Douglas Bader. The unit would have a new role too, one more to Babbage's liking. Fruitless day and night patrols, and very occasional interceptions of lone bombers were a thing of the past. Defensive operations would be replaced by circuses and rhubarbs (low-level patrols, usually under cloud cover, seeking targets of opportunity in France, Belgium and the Netherlands). In many ways this approach represented a reversal of the Battle of Britain. The RAF would now be on the offensive, fighting over enemy territory, albeit with the associated disadvantages: flak, fighter opposition, shortage of fuel and the risk of capture for anyone shot down. But in his own quiet way, Babbage relished the challenge.

He'd be flying a new aircraft too. With 602 he flew the Mk I Spitfire;[115] initially with 41 it was the Mk II, which offered only limited improvements. A slightly more powerful engine gave a better rate of climb and service ceiling but there was a minor penalty in terms of top speed. Now, though, he'd be operating the uprated Mk Va and Vb. The key to their improved performance was a new, more powerful engine, the Merlin 45. It was fitted with a single-stage supercharger that increased performance at height (up to around 20,000ft) and a new carburettor. The latter overcame the problem of fuel starvation during zero-G manoeuvres that plagued the early Spitfires and left them at a disadvantage against the Me 109. This latest model was certainly a match for the new Me 109F, although it would prove inferior to the Focke-Wulf (Fw) 190 when it was introduced – an event in which Babbage would play a significant part. The key difference between the Mk Va and Vb was their armament. The Vb boasted greater firepower: two Hispano 7.92mm cannons in place of four of the original eight machine guns.

As Babbage and his colleagues prepared to face their latest challenge, it's illuminating to reflect on the make-up of his new squadron. Against a pilot establishment of 12 officers and 11 NCOs, there were seven officers and 17 NCOs. It wasn't just balance that was lacking. It was the evident lack of experience. Other than Babbage, only six pilots had seen combat during the Battle of Britain and roughly half had seen no action at all. It was a situation that owed everything to the need to rest exhausted aircrew and make good Battle of Britain losses – a testing challenge for the man soon to replace Donald Finlay. With the CO promoted and posted, Squadron Leader Lionel 'Elmer' Gaunce,[116] a Canadian, would take over on 9 August. He'd been flying with the squadron as a supernumerary pilot since 29 July; this followed more than a month in a similar role at Kenley after a period of hospitalisation.[117]

Operations at Merston began quietly. On 30 July the CO led a pair of aircraft on an uneventful patrol in the Selsey Bill area. Offensive operations in the shape of rhubarbs across the Channel began on 1 August with the emphasis on blooding the newer pilots. However, bad weather that day prevented any penetration into enemy territory. The first sorties over France came next day with strikes recorded on a variety of targets: vessels, trains and rail facilities, factories, piers loaded with stores, and what was thought to be a searchlight post. Most of these early targets were on or close to the French coast in an area centred on Dieppe, some 100 miles south-east of Merston. Babbage's first rhubarb, a one-hour 30-minute sortie, came on 3 August. With Flight Sergeant George Swanwick as his No. 2, his was one of only two pairs to fly that day thanks to poor weather. They crossed the coast at Le Tréport and attacked a train before heading inland for a sweep from Abbeville to Dieppe. Swanwick also strafed a boat, only to find himself engaged by flak, albeit inaccurate. For those coming under fire for the first time, accurate or not, flak usually had the desired effect and discouraged further attacks.

Babbage's next sortie, on 7 August, brought frustration. Sent to patrol Selsey Bill for just over an hour, he missed the main action of the day. In his absence 12 aircraft, led by the CO, took part in Circus 62. Six Blenheim bombers, escorted by 17 fighter squadrons from 11 Group, attacked a power station at Lille in the Pas-de-Calais. To rub salt into a festering wound, together with 610 and 616 Squadrons, part of the Tangmere Wing led by Douglas Bader and allocated to target support, 41 Squadron saw most of the action. On the credit side of the Merston ledger, Sergeant Herbert Mitchell, a New Zealander, claimed a damaged Me 109F. But there was a debit entry too: the squadron's first loss. Flight Lieutenant Gilbert Draper, OC B Flight, was shot down. Attacked by an Me 109F and with his aircraft on fire, he was forced to bail out over enemy territory near Merville. Despite suffering from minor burns, he managed to enjoy a single day of freedom before capture; he then spent the rest of the war as a prisoner. In a postscript to the squadron's first Merston circus, and Wing Commander Donald Finlay's last sortie with 41, the 12 Group rear support wing was led by Wing Commander Bob Stanford Tuck. His two claims that day, an Me 109F destroyed and Me 109E probable, were the last he would ever make.[118]

Babbage's first circus operation came two days later, but Circus 68 was not a success. Together with the Kenley Wing (452, 485 and 602 Squadrons), the Tangmere Wing was allocated to target support for five Blenheims attacking Gosnay power station in the Pas-de-Calais. Led for the first time by the new CO, the squadron failed to rendezvous over Westhampnett with the Spitfires of 610 and 616 Squadrons. By the time Squadron Leader Gaunce had 41 Squadron airborne and in formation they were some 20 miles behind their Tangmere colleagues. He nevertheless pressed on to the French coast and flew some 30 miles inland from Le Touquet at 29,000ft before returning. After a descent to 20,000ft, Babbage saw a number of Me 109s coming down behind the formation, which led to a short but indecisive engagement before all 12 aircraft returned safely to Merston.

There was one notable who failed to return safely that day, Douglas Bader. Twenty-four hours later he was reported as a POW. The only certainty about his demise was that he bailed out. Controversy over the reason why has continued to rage, albeit there is a plausible theory that this controversial individual, a man who divided opinion then as now, was the inadvertent victim of a friendly-fire incident. In a final addition to a roll call of the famous that day, a certain Pilot Officer Johnnie Johnson, who would later become the RAF's top-scoring ace, was flying with Tangmere's 616 Squadron and claimed both a confirmed and a probable Me 109; the former was his fifth kill.

Two more circus operations followed for Babbage on 12 August. The first, Circus 70, was a return to Gosnay power station as target support for six Hampdens. After Bader's loss, the Tangmere Wing was led by a familiar face, Wing Commander Don Finlay. It proved a costly morning for 41 Squadron. A number of Me 109s seen earlier crossing ahead of the formation but then lost in the sun, later approached from behind and picked off Sergeants Alan Bull and Raymond Chapman. Bull bailed out unharmed and was captured near St Omer; he would spend the rest of the war as a POW. Chapman, however, was wounded and after bailing out safely near Lille he suffered the same fate as his colleague: incarceration.

Babbage's second circus took place in the early evening, a raid by six Blenheims on the Le Trait shipbuilding yards in Haute-Normandie. For Circus 71 the Tangmere Wing was assigned the escort cover role, albeit with depleted contributions from 610 and 616 Squadrons: a composite unit of four and eight aircraft respectively that saw no action. The excitement was confined to 41 on their return from the raid, about ten miles off the coast near Dieppe. A number of Luftwaffe fighters were seen well below, apparently stalking the bombers on their return. In the subsequent action Flight Lieutenant Roy Marples and Pilot Officer Williams were credited with a shared Me 109.

The norm was to launch 12 aircraft on a circus operation. However, Babbage was one of only ten 41 Squadron aircraft assigned to Circus 72 on the afternoon of 14 August: a raid by 12 Blenheims on E-boats in Boulogne harbour. Together with the Hornchurch Wing, Tangmere was tasked in the support role – led this time by Tangmere's newly arrived Wing Commander, Henry Woodhouse.[119] On a significant day both for Babbage and for his squadron, during a relatively lengthy sortie of one hour 35 minutes the young pilot officer would make his first claim at Merston – but 41 would lose its second flight commander in a week.

En route to Boulogne, 610 Squadron was vectored to the St Omer area where they engaged with some 40 Me 109Es and 109Fs, leaving 41 to continue to the target area. There they were vectored north-east at 25,000ft on a sweep to Gravelines. Babbage, in the lead section with Sergeant Arthur Glen as his No. 2, saw two Me 109s tailing the section on his port side. Immediately he broke away and made a diving attack on one of the enemy fighters. With no option but to approach from the beam, it was a difficult deflection shot.

Unsurprisingly, his bullets failed to find their mark, a disappointment exacerbated by a cannon stoppage. Glen was still with him as he pulled away to reposition for another attack, but lost sight of the German fighters in the sun. A third 109 then joined the other two as they turned their attention on his leader. Babbage now had his hands full, 'heavily engaged' for a time. Life became marginally easier for him when the third 109 broke off to attack his No. 2. It proved a fateful decision. After one ineffective burst when Glen saw tracer pass harmlessly down his port side, the German dived away, descending from 22,000 to 10,000ft. There he made the cardinal error of flying straight and level, allowing Glen the chance gradually to overhaul and dispose of him from directly astern.

As Glen's victim bailed out, Babbage was manoeuvring into position for a three-second burst at one of the two remaining Me 109s in a gentle turn. As his de Wilde rounds[120] struck home, the enemy fighter's engine began to belch white glycol smoke and it dived away steeply towards the French coast. Following it down would be a fool's errand – the remaining 109 was continuing to show interest in him, and from behind too. His only option was to turn hard, offering his pursuer a fleeting opportunity for a high deflection shot. It was enough to see the German fighter roll away and disappear below him. Time to go home, he thought. A damaged and a confirmed represented a pretty good return from a three-on-two engagement after more than an hour-and-a-half in the air.

There was no such luck for OC A Flight, Flight Lieutenant Archie Winskill.[121] His unusual story is worth a brief digression. After destroying an Me 109, he was hit by cannon fire from behind. With his canopy gone and enveloped in black smoke, his aircraft went into a spin from which it was impossible to recover – his damaged flying controls were simply ineffective. With no option but to bail out, he delayed his exit until as low as he dared to reduce the chances of being seen. He landed mid-afternoon near a small hamlet, Sainte-Marie-Kerque, some 5–6 miles south of Gravelines, where he was hidden and helped by a French farming family. Thus began a lengthy period of escape and evasion, culminating in his eventual return to England on 23 November. As one of the first to return using the Pat Line[122] via Spain and Gibraltar, he was never allowed to fly over France again lest he were captured, tortured and revealed his knowledge of the escape route. But Winskill's story doesn't end there – nor do the coincidences.

Early 1943 found Squadron Leader Winskill commanding 232 Squadron in North Africa. On 18 January he was shot down once again; he bailed out from his doomed Spitfire and landed in the sea off the North African coast. From there, with the help of a few Arabs, he managed to return safely to his squadron, thus becoming one of the very few during the war to return twice from behind enemy lines. Unwittingly, he'd also become the 51st victim of Erich Rudorffer, the man who had shot down his erstwhile colleague Nigel Keable some five months before.

A month or so earlier, on 20 December 1942, the author's father became Rudorffer's 47th victim – two days after he'd been in a dogfight with the very same man, albeit unknowingly. Saving the life of his No. 2 that day, Sergeant Roy Hussey, cost Pilot Officer 'Robbie' Robertson an eye. It also brought to a premature end the flying career of a Spitfire ace who'd served under Squadron Leader Winskill when 72 Squadron briefly came under the latter's command at Ayr in August 1942. He was covering for Squadron Leader 'Bobby' Oxspring,[123] otherwise engaged on the Dieppe Raid. To complete these linkages, in less than two months' time a certain Flight Lieutenant R.W. Oxspring would take over as Babbage's flight commander.

The next sortie Babbage flew, on 17 August, showed just how easily things could go wrong. The Tangmere Wing was in the escort role for Circus 76, a raid by six Blenheims on the docks at Le Havre. With the bombers at 11,000ft, 616 Squadron provided top cover 5,000ft above, while 41 and 610 flew 2,000ft below. One Blenheim was soon lagging the formation and turned for home. Not long afterwards, roughly 50 miles off the English coast, the lead Blenheim lost its starboard engine and it too turned back. Although the bombing mission was aborted, the escort squadrons pressed on towards the French coast before they in turn were recalled. For Babbage and his colleagues, indeed for the entire Tangmere Wing, it was a frustrating sortie. First came the surge of adrenalin as landfall approached, eyes everywhere, searching for enemy fighters. Then the let-down of a recall. No time to relax, though. If anything, the danger actually increased now. Heading for the safety of home, metaphorical guard down, potentially they were easy meat for Luftwaffe fighters diving down from out of the sun. It was time to follow another of Sailor Malan's ten rules: 'Always keep a sharp lookout . . .'. After gearing himself for action that never came, Babbage felt a strange combination of frustration, disappointment and relief. And to make matters worse, he would miss much of the excitement to come. The next day's circus represented a stiff challenge to Gaunce's relatively inexperienced squadron.

On 18 August the Tangmere Wing was tasked as target support for Circus 78, a raid by nine Blenheims on a familiar target, the engineering works at Lille. As they made landfall the fleeting appearance of a number of Me 109s destroyed the integrity of the combined formations and 41 Squadron was forced to break away, leaving 610 and 616 to continue on to Lille. It was just what the Messerschmitts wanted. When they reappeared moments later, diving down behind the rearmost aircraft, a major dogfight ensued with Spitfires outnumbered more than 3:1. In the circumstances the outcome was better than it might have been: two probable Me 109Fs and four damaged – but at a cost.

Sergeant Richard Jury was shot down and killed while Pilot Officer Mark Williams was captured after suffering a similar fate. Williams had been flying Spitfires for barely four months, while Jury was one of the squadron's more experienced individuals. He'd served previously with 616 and 603 Squadrons but was flying his first sortie after seven days' war leave. It's impossible to know whether this had any bearing on his demise. What we do know is that flying is a perishable skill. Equally, the demands of operations were such that regular breaks were essential. Balancing these competing pressures was a function of leadership – leadership exercised by individuals who, by virtue of their position, suffered the very same pressures in even greater measure. All of which suggests that the recognition and respect for Fighter Command's young paladins engendered by Churchill's stirring words should extend far beyond the summer of 1940 – and beyond Fighter Command too for that matter. These philosophical meanderings provide the backdrop to Babbage's own departure on 19 August to begin seven days' war leave. It meant he would miss his squadron's involvement in a unique event.

When Bader bailed out of his stricken Spitfire, he was forced to leave one of his artificial legs behind. It's hard to imagine just how difficult that made the subsequent parachute landing, on just a single prosthesis; but that's what this gritty individual accomplished. It's no surprise that he damaged his remaining artificial leg in the process. Bader was hospitalised briefly in St Omer and, astonishingly, managed to escape briefly before being recaptured. Equally amazing were the subsequent arrangements between the Luftwaffe and the RAF, whereby a replacement artificial right leg for Bader would be delivered on 19 August. Safe passage for the mission was offered to St Omer where the prosthesis was to be dropped by parachute. Those taking part in this operation, Circus 81 (Operation Leg), planned to fly on afterwards and bomb the target for the very mission on which Bader was lost ten days earlier, Gosnay power station. In retrospect, this not only seems less than prudent – forewarned, the Germans could track the raid's progress – it also appears to offend the cooperative spirit behind these humanitarian arrangements. That said, both sides clearly accepted that once the leg was delivered any temporary truce no longer applied.

The first part of Operation Leg was accomplished when one of six Blenheims from 18 Squadron, flying at 10,000ft west of the airfield at St Omer, released a specially constructed wooden crate, marked with Red Cross symbols, containing Bader's new artificial leg; it landed by parachute at a nearby village, Quiestède. Tangmere's role in all this was as escort to the Blenheims with the wing leader, Wing Commander Woodhouse, responsible for advising the Tangmere controller, 'Leg gone', once he saw the parachute open. It seems somehow fitting that cloud cover meant none of the bombers was able to complete their mission that day. Meanwhile, 41 Squadron's 11 Spitfires returned safely having seen little sign of the Luftwaffe once Operation Leg was complete. Those few fighters they did see showed little appetite for the fight. The Blenheims were less fortunate. Forced down below 1,000ft by low cloud, they met heavy flak crossing the French coast. All six were hit but there was only a single casualty: a wounded observer. The other four supporting wings on Circus 81, Biggin Hill, Hornchurch, Kenley and Northolt, fared worse. Eight aircraft and four pilots were lost; one was wounded and another ended up as a POW – this in return for claims of nine Me 109s destroyed, five probables and five damaged.

Babbage's first operation on return from leave was on 26 August. Three things that happened during his absence are worth recounting. First, leading the Tangmere Wing in an offensive sweep as part of a circus operation on 21 August, Wing Commander Woodhouse reported seeing an aircraft he didn't recognise. It had square wings with broader tips and a larger tailfin than the Me 109E. Little did he realise it was Tangmere's first sighting of the Luftwaffe's latest fighter, the Fw 190. The following day saw an equally unusual occurrence, a 'by invitation' appearance in one of 41 Squadron's Spitfires by Flight Lieutenant Colin Gray.[124] The man who would go on to become New Zealand's highest-scoring fighter pilot shot down an Me 109 during a rhubarb to the Le Havre–Le Tréport area. At the time Gray had 16 confirmed kills to his credit, all flying the Spitfire. Now, though, he was flying Hurricanes with 1 Squadron, but somehow persuaded Elmer Gaunce to include him in a 13-aircraft sweep led by the Tangmere wing commander!

This incident says a good deal about the calibre of individual who succeeded in the air combat arena. Those like Gray who combined supreme flying ability with deadly marksmanship – Sailor Malan and Johnnie Johnson for example – were a rare breed. Rarer still were those with the New Zealander's appetite for the fight, a readiness actively to seek out the dangers of engagement with the enemy. That said, Gray's situation was unusual. His twin brother, Kenneth, a bomber pilot and one of the first New Zealanders to be awarded a DFC, joined the RAF before him. Colin was delayed in New Zealand after failing the medical his brother passed. Ken Gray had been killed nearly 16 months earlier. Ironically, he was en route from his base in Scotland to visit Colin in a Whitley when he flew into a hill on 1 May 1940. Deeply affected by the loss of his twin, it's a moot point whether this tragedy affected Colin Gray's attitude towards risk.

The third incident during Babbage's absence is of little significance in itself, but worthy of mention because of what it says about life on an operational squadron. It also adds context to some of the previously noted but unexplained personnel movements. He returned to find that on 22 August Sergeant Frank Watson had been posted to 19 Squadron, part of 12 Group at Coltishall, little more than five weeks after his arrival from the Grangemouth OTU. What lay behind such short-term postings was often a 'last in, first out' policy. When a squadron suffered significant losses, the upshot was usually a call from Group HQ to other, better populated units asking them to provide replacements forthwith. Indeed, there was just such a request shortly before Babbage left 602 Squadron. The resulting cascade of movements, inevitably involving the least experienced aircrew, did little for those involved, let alone squadron cohesion. In this case 41 would lose an individual barely operational and in all likelihood see him eventually replaced by someone even less experienced.

Babbage returned to an uneventful 11-aircraft sweep on 26 August, another lengthy sortie at one hour 45 minutes. The Tangmere Wing acted in the target support role for Circus 87, an attack by six Blenheims on the airfield at St Omer. Orbiting the target while the bombers set about their task, they met a dozen Me 109s closing fast, head-on some 2,000 feet below. Neither formation reacted. Like a similar encounter involving 616's Spitfires moments later, these incidents perfectly illustrate the stage the conflict had reached. As a general rule, neither side would engage in squadron level fighter-v-fighter combat without numerical or positional advantage, and ideally both. There were, of course, exceptions: protection either of bombers or fighter colleagues, for example. But neither applied that day.

Next day, another long sortie was anything but uneventful. A circus on the morning of 27 August saw Wing Commander Woodhouse leading the Tangmere Wing at the head of 41 Squadron with Babbage in the CO's three-aircraft section. Things went wrong from the start of what was effectively a combined operation. Together with the Biggin Hill Wing, Tangmere would be part of the target support package for five Blenheims bombing St Omer again. But Circus 85 was simply a diversionary operation for Circus 86, almost an hour later: 12 Blenheims supported by 11 fighter squadrons for an attack on Lille power station. To illustrate the complexity of a difficult operation where strict routing and timing applied, squadrons from the Northolt escort wing were to fly at 14,000, 15,000 and 17,000ft, with Kenley's escort cover at 18,000, 20,000 and 22,000ft respectively. The Biggin Hill Wing would follow the main formation out at 25,000–30,000ft, while the Tangmere squadrons would be at the same altitude in the target area and cover the returning bombers. The reality was somewhat different.

It started with the bombers. Initially only three appeared at the designated RV, well ahead of schedule. A fourth followed later but failed to join up, and there was no sign of the fifth Blenheim. With the bombers reduced to a token force and fighter wings operating independently of their charges, the raid was abandoned. This left the Northolt and Kenley Wings to fight their way back. Meanwhile the Tangmere Wing had reached St Omer, where Woodhouse led an attack on 14–18 Me 109Fs, diving down on them as they approached from the south-west in twos and threes. In the ensuing dogfights, Babbage managed two or three 'squirts' as black and white crosses appeared fleetingly in his sights. Protecting his leader, the CO, was his prime concern. In doing so he saw pieces fly off one aircraft Gaunce fired at, justifying his claim for a damaged. Meanwhile the other member of his section, Sergeant 'Bill' Brew, was engaged with a separate aircraft. Gaunce saw the Australian's rounds strike home on the Me 109 from close range before he lost control of his aircraft. Brew's Spitfire had been badly damaged by an unseen assailant – it was always the way. With no option but to bail out, he landed safely near St Omer but would spend the rest of the war as a prisoner.

The upshot of a frenzied operation and 41 Squadron's harassed return from France was the loss of 19-year-old Sergeant Harry Morgan – his body would eventually be picked up from the Channel – and two further claims, both to Sergeant Wilfred 'Bill' Palmer: a confirmed and a damaged Me 109F. Despite the aborted attack on St Omer, 11 Group counted Circus 85 a success. By drawing in large numbers of enemy fighters it succeeded in its primary aim, that of creating a diversion for Circus 86.

The three days before Babbage flew again on operations were uncharacteristically quiet, which is probably just as well given what was to come. There were just a few convoy patrols, plus a single rhubarb which cost another life. On 28 August, six aircraft, led by the CO, chanced on some Me 109 activity in the vicinity of the airfield at Le Havre-Octeville. In the engagements that followed, Squadron Leader Gaunce damaged one enemy fighter but lost contact with his No. 2, Sergeant Bodkin. He then found himself being harassed by three or four Messerschmitts. Desperately needing to shake them off, he flew west as low as he dared, turning hard round a farmhouse, hurtling across a few fields and then dropping down the cliffs to sea level. Once he reached the Channel, he realised he was on his own. There he flew up and down just off the coast, hoping to join up with others from his formation. But he couldn't afford to wait long. When no one appeared, and there were no responses to his radio calls, he headed north for Merston. It was only after others from his formation landed that he realised there was no sign of his No. 2. Sergeant Fred Bodkin Royal Canadian Air Force (RCAF) had been killed. And Gaunce had been more fortunate than he realised. His Spitfire, W3374, had suffered 'Cat[egory] C' damage; repairs were beyond the scope of Tangmere's resources. It would require outside assistance eventually to recover an aircraft that would soon feature in a tragic accident.

Compensation for this latest fatality came in the shape of three replacements, posted in on 29 August. That made five new pilots, young and raw, who'd arrived in the past three days – all of whom would have to be brought quickly up to speed in a challenging environment. The strain this put on the older hands was graphically illustrated on 31 August, a day when the squadron flew three 12-aircraft offensive sweeps. The first took off at 0535, the last landed at 2005. Babbage was one of seven who flew on all three of these operations – four-and-a-half hours in total. For people like him, whose very survival depended on their wits, on their reactions, this represented a dangerously long working day. So how did things turn out?

The first launch proved a non-event. The Tangmere Wing was tasked with supporting a navy operation, Iliad: a pair of destroyers hunting for submarines operating in the Channel. Squadron Leader Gaunce's formation joined the other two Tangmere squadrons, 129 and 616, overhead base, but within ten minutes of setting course for their operating area he'd lost sight of them. The CO was then ordered to return to base. All that 41 Squadron achieved from this abortive effort was a first operational sortie for Sergeant Cyril Whiteford, a Rhodesian.

Babbage's second sortie was in support of Circus 90: six Blenheims tasked against St Omer airfield, for the fourth time that month. Together with the Biggin Hill squadrons, a reduced Tangmere Wing – just 41 and 616 Squadrons – was allocated the target support role. Both wings passed up the chance of Me 109 engagements on sensible grounds: they were poorly positioned relative to the enemy aircraft. Given that 41 was blooding two more newcomers, Flight Lieutenant Leslie Bache and Sergeant Peter Hind, this was no bad thing.

A return to the shipyards at Le Trait was Babbage's final sortie of the day, Circus 92. Together with the two Tangmere squadrons, 41 was tasked as escort for six Blenheims. All went well until the return after an uneventful, unmolested but largely ineffective bombing run. The damage wrought by two dozen 250lb bombs wasn't even enough to disrupt work the following day. Gaunce's formation fell into a well-laid trap. Sighting two unidentified aircraft up-sun, he ordered the squadron to break up – just as three Me 109s suddenly appeared below them. Almost at once, Sergeant Peter Hind was shot down from behind, his aircraft engulfed in flames. As the others turned to face their attackers, several individual dogfights began. In one of these Sergeant Charles Valiquet RCAF found himself receiving close attention from a number of enemy fighters and was lucky to escape – at a cost though.

His damaged aircraft would never make it back to base, so he elected to carry out a crash landing at West Wittering, eight miles or so south-west of Merston. To add to the Canadian's disappointment, his claim of a destroyed Me 109F was reduced to a probable. Babbage had an equally fortunate escape. He was hit by cannon and machine-gun fire which damaged his port wing, blew away the flaps and riddled his aircraft with shrapnel. With no airspeed indicator either, he then burst a tyre on landing. It could have been a lot worse.

Valiquet's was the squadron's only success – scant compensation for the missing Sergeant Hind. He'd been with 41 barely a week and this was only his second operational sortie (his first was less than six hours earlier). Badly burned before he bailed out of his doomed aircraft, he was hospitalised on landing; he would never recover and died from his wounds in captivity 11 months later. Hind's demise offers support for a metric dating from the Battle of Britain. Those who survived their first three operational sorties stood a better than even chance of surviving the battle itself; and those who did that stood a similar chance of surviving the war. Put another way, pilots new to operations were six times more likely to be shot down than their more experienced colleagues.[125]

Thus drew to a close one of the most intensive months in the squadron's history, and this despite ten days on which there was no operational flying whatsoever. Ten aircraft were lost and three pilots killed; six became POWs while a seventh (Archie Winskill) was making good his eventual escape – not that his colleagues were aware, of course. Sadder still, of those captured two were wounded, one of whom would later die in captivity. In purely statistical terms, Babbage was fortunate to emerge from August unscathed – an achievement that owes a good deal to his ability and experience. Despite a week's leave, he'd added another 14 sorties and nearly 20 operational hours to his logbook and been through a lot. What, he wondered, after all this, do the coming weeks and months hold?

Not much initially, was the short answer – other than continuation of the regular personnel movements, both in and out. Pilot Officer Raymond Sly, another Australian who'd arrived on 29 August, was posted out just three days later without having flown a single operational sortie. The likeliest explanation was to locate him with his fellow countrymen on 452 Squadron. Although nominally an Australian unit, it contained a mix of nationalities.

The few patrols the squadron flew during the first few days of September were ideal for giving the influx of new men time in the air. The first piece of excitement, an offensive sweep as part of Circus 93, came on 4 September. Babbage was one of the 12 who took part, led by the CO. The Tangmere Wing was cast in the rear support role for a late afternoon raid by 12 Blenheims on Mazingarbe power station in the Pas-de-Calais. It was a major undertaking, with 19 squadrons involved. While 41 Squadron's participation was 'completely uneventful', the claims and losses from others who took part were substantial. Seven Me 109s were confirmed destroyed, ten were probables and five damaged. Losses were one bomber and seven fighters; four men were killed, four captured and one wounded.

For more than a fortnight things were then remarkably quiet – just the odd rhubarb and convoy patrol. But by 16 September, with Babbage having flown just that single 90-minute sortie, Gaunce had had enough and organised a practice combat exercise. In this, two four-aircraft formations were to be attacked by a pair of aircraft, one of which was being flown by Sergeant Hunt. Some 15 minutes into the exercise his aircraft was seen in a steeply descending port turn at around 5,000ft, above a layer of cloud. Sergeant Glen watched in amazement as black smoke suddenly belched from the engine (it appeared to have stopped), whereupon the aircraft flicked violently and the port wing broke off. Hunt stood no chance. His body was eventually recovered, while the wreckage of his aircraft, W3374, was found scattered across a minefield on Littlehampton beach; the detached wing landed separately on a road.

The subsequent Accidents Investigation Branch (AIB) report[126] notes that 'the accident was caused by structural failure of the port mainplane during violent aerobatic manoeuvres'. However, it concedes that: 'It has not been possible to determine the exact sequence of the break-up as much of the wreckage landed in a coastal minefield and the parts which were eventually recovered had been seriously damaged by fire.' It goes on to state that: 'The primary failure occurred in the port mainplane, the front spar failing 5ft outboard of the root attachment bolts.' Although there's no indication of what lay behind the failure, the report offers a supposition: 'The fact that the pilot found himself about to dive into cloud before his blind-flying instruments had a chance to settle may have led to harsh handling of the controls and serious overstressing.'

W3374 was the same aircraft that suffered Cat 3 damage during Gaunce's lucky escape on 28 August. Could there possibly have been a connection between this incident and Hunt's accident? It seems surprising that the AIB report contains no mention of the aircraft's prior history, if only to rule out the possibility of a causal connection. While it concedes the impossibility of determining 'the exact sequence of the break-up', its conclusions draw heavily on third party visual evidence of questionable value. It would have been well-nigh impossible for an observer to determine the precise sequence of events that occurred within fractions of a second and at a distance. The nature of the exercise in which the observer was engaged, nerves at a stretch, offers support for this view and leads to a question. Could the sequence of events have been different from that reported? What if the main spar failure were the cause, rather than the effect, of the violent flick manoeuvre seen by the observer? And if this were the case, could prior damage have been a contributory factor? Sadly, we will never know. Speculation apart, it should be acknowledged that Hunt's accident was neither the first nor the last of its type. Babbage's 602 Squadron colleague, Sergeant Brian Bailey, had been killed in broadly similar circumstances on 30 December 1939, when the wing reportedly detached from his aircraft during aerobatics near Drem. And on 27 January 1942, Sergeant 'Pat' Rusk, from 222 Squadron at North Weald, died in similar circumstances during an air test.[127]

Returning to Babbage, he was back in the cockpit three times on 17 September: a morning convoy patrol, then barely time to catch his breath between back-to-back offensive sweeps in the afternoon and early evening – just over four hours' flying in all. For the first sweep, Circus 95, the Tangmere Wing was in the forward support role for a repeat attack by 24 Blenheims on the Mazingarbe power station. Approaching the target area Babbage saw more than 30 enemy aircraft orbiting in the distance, but they failed to materialise into a threat. At around 20,000ft the CO peeled off to attack two Me 109s, seeing enough smoke from one during his firing pass to claim a damaged – only to find himself attacked by another pair, which he did well to shake off. The only other incident of note cost Sergeant Glen two weeks off flying with damaged eardrums. The controls on W3719 froze at 25,000ft. Unable to regain control of his plunging aircraft until it reached 2,000ft, he was lucky to survive a frightening experience. And it would be 15 days before his aircraft flew its next operation.

Babbage had just 90 minutes between landing from the power station mission and his next take-off. It was back to work with a vengeance, albeit once again there was little to show for the wing's target support role in Circus 96, an aborted raid by six Hampdens. They couldn't find the Marquise munitions factory in the Pas-de-Calais. All 41 Squadron found on their return from an otherwise uneventful sortie was very heavy flack at 26,000ft just inland from Le Touquet, at Étaples. Next day, 18 September, would prove more fruitful – the squadron's busiest day since the Battle of Britain.

After an early take-off as part of a 12-aircraft formation, Babbage landed at Manston for a briefing on his first 'Roadsted', a fighter operation against shipping. In concert with the Hurricanes of 615 Squadron, 41 was to provide cover for three Blenheims attacking a large tanker off Blankenberge on the Belgian coast. Six Spitfires from 91 Squadron were detailed as top cover but they failed to materialise. The operation was further compromised when 41 Squadron lost contact with the Hurricanes and Blenheims thanks to thick haze below a 3,000ft cloudbase. In one sense it mattered not because the Blenheims almost certainly sunk their target, despite the attention of several supporting flak ships. But by now the German defences had been alerted and some 20 Luftwaffe fighters soon appeared on the scene to play havoc with both the bombers and their escort. Two Blenheims were shot down and a third damaged, while two Hurricanes were also lost. Short of ammunition after attacking the flak ships, they nevertheless accounted for one German fighter and damaged three more. The Spitfires of 41 and 91 Squadrons were badly missed. Babbage and his colleagues, however, were otherwise engaged.

Finding themselves near Ostend, some ten miles away, Gaunce's formation caught a number of aircraft unawares in the vicinity of an airfield. But they were then subject to the attention of several aggressive Luftwaffe fighters, alerted to the plight of the tanker. In the engagements that followed, eight pilots between them claimed five aircraft destroyed and two probables, both Me 109Es. The destroyed aircraft were a mixed bag comprising two Me 109Fs, a Ju W34,[128] a Gotha Go 145[129] and a Fw 190. The last of these – the first Fw 190 ever to be shot down – fell to Babbage. It's quite a story. But first, to give a flavour of some desperately close encounters that morning, Sergeant Bill Palmer takes up the tale:

> "Escorting Blenheims attacking supply ship off Ostend, Ju 52 recognised.[130] Saw enemy aircraft in flames after stern attack by Spitfire, afterwards seen to be Sergeant Whiteford. Returning with Sergeant Whiteford, afterwards saw three radial-engined fighters to port, turned to engage but enemy aircraft disappeared into low cloud. Set course 240 degrees for home, as bombers had left. After crossing water for some time, Sergeant Whiteford and self crossed a coastline which did not seem familiar. Unable to identify landmarks, flew inland and saw four aircraft to starboard which Sergeant Whiteford said were Airacobras. I was suspicious and told him to turn to port, as he was about 400 yards away. At that, I saw his guns firing and immediately recognised the aircraft as 109Fs. Fuel was short and, being hopelessly lost, I turned towards Sergeant Whiteford and engaged the enemy aircraft. I saw Sergeant Whiteford pass beneath me in the opposite direction, and then I was too busy with the enemy aircraft.
>
> "I fired several bursts as we were dogfighting, and then saw two further enemy aircraft coming up. Altogether there were five around me, and the sixth was being chased by Sergeant Whiteford. I flew down the main street of a small town for evasive action, but this did not stop the enemy aircraft from firing. I turned round completely several times and the enemy aircraft would split up and climb away then, apparently not relishing a dogfight. I had by then given up all hope of returning and just concentrated on trying to knock someone down. I found myself flying straight for some high-tension cables. Being at zero feet I had no option but to fly underneath. I immediately pulled up into a steep climbing turn and saw a large sheet of flame. The nearest '109 had gone into the cables and blown up. I received a cannon shell hit on my right

> boot and several hits in the fuel tank, which started to leak. I turned into the enemy aircraft again and they scattered. About ten miles out, two of the enemy aircraft had turned back and then the third broke away, leaving one. I turned inside this one as he attacked me from slightly above and astern. I was on his tail in two complete turns and opened fire with my remaining rounds of machine gun. I saw hits, and he climbed to about 200 feet and fired a red Very light, then turned on his side and the last I saw was him going slowly towards the sea. I was then 20 miles from the French coast and I steered due north climbing very slowly. I called for homing on Button D and heard ground station say that I was 30 miles due south of Shoreham. I ran out of fuel seven miles off Friston and, owing to lack of height, crash-landed in sea. Picked up by launch."

The upshot of this combat report was that Sergeant Palmer was credited with one Me 109 destroyed plus another probable. These successes brought to an end a remarkable few weeks for a man who had joined his first squadron only seven months earlier. Including these two successes, between 18 August and 18 September he was credited with three Me 109Fs destroyed, a probable and two damaged. A month later he was awarded the DFM and commissioned – just rewards for a man who epitomised the spirit of a special generation. He went on to become a flight commander and was still serving with the squadron on 10 April 1942, the day his luck ran out. Shot down off Boulogne, he bailed out and spent the rest of the war as a prisoner.

CHAPTER 12

HAUPTMANN WALTER ADOLPH, GRUPPENKOMMANDEUR

On 4 October 1940, Hauptmann Walter Adolph was appointed Gruppenkommandeur II. Gruppe, Jagdgeschwader 26 'Schlageter'.[131] Less than six weeks later, on 13 November, he was awarded the Knight's Cross, in part for his leadership of II. Gruppe.

On 21 August 1941, when the new Tangmere Wing leader, Henry Woodhouse, saw an aircraft he couldn't identify – different from the Me 109s he was familiar with – he had no idea of the threat it would pose to the Mk V Spitfire his squadrons flew. He was equally unaware that the aircraft itself, a Fw 190A, had already proved its superiority. Five days before, a combined formation of Fw 190s and Me 109s claimed four Spitfires in an early morning engagement near Boulogne. One of these fell to the guns of Hauptmann Walter Adolph.

Once Erprobungsstaffel 190, the unit responsible for operational testing of the Fw 190A, moved from Rechlin in Germany to Le Bourget, near Paris, around the end of July 1941, Adolph's Gruppe was the first to convert to the new aircraft and witness the advantages it brought. Suddenly the Luftwaffe had a fighter that could not only compete with the Spitfire, it could outperform it in almost every way: rate of climb, roll rate, top speed and firepower, where it boasted four 20mm cannon and two 7.9mm heavy machine guns. Only in terms of turn rate – a critically important factor in aerial combat – was the Spitfire superior. That said, even if a Fw pilot were being outturned by a Spitfire behind him, he could escape by rapidly reversing the direction of turn and diving away, a manoeuvre even an alert Spitfire pilot would find difficult to follow.

On the morning of 18 September 1941, Adolph climbed into his Fw 190A, quickly strapped in and started the powerful BMW 801 radial engine. He was about to take off on his 79th operational sortie, leading an eight-aircraft *Alarmstart* (scramble) in response to a call for assistance from a vessel under attack just off Blankenberge. The seasoned veteran had no way of knowing he was about to come up against a squadron he'd encountered before.

Nearly a year earlier, on 11 October 1940, Adolph was flying one of around 50 Me 109s which engaged 41 Squadron over Kent. The German fighters were well placed. At over 30,000ft they were a good 4,000ft above their prey. Using a classic Luftwaffe ruse, the leader of Adolph's formation sent three aircraft diving down through the Spitfires as a decoy, leaving him and his four companions to attack the rear of the formation. It was all too easy. Adolph had time to pick his target and closed on the unsuspecting rearmost man, Pilot Officer John Lecky. An extended burst of fire quickly sent the 19 year old's aircraft down in flames. Lecky bailed out but was found dead in his parachute at Preston Hall, Maidstone. His training at the RAF College Cranwell cut short by the war, he'd been with the squadron just nine days, living what he described in a letter to his parents shortly before he was killed as 'the life I love'. He was Adolph's tenth victory of the war.

Adolph's record includes another Spitfire destroyed in this same engagement, but it's a questionable claim. 41 Squadron lost only three aircraft that day – the other two resulted from a mid-air collision; one pilot parachuted to safety, the other was killed. Such examples illustrate why there are questions over the final tally of Experten like Adolph. His operational career began with the Condor Legion during the Spanish Civil War. Flying an early Messerschmitt, the 109B, he claimed his first victim on 1 December 1937, a Republican Polikarpov I-15 (a Russian biplane). Flying with 2./JG 1, he opened his World War II account on 1 October 1939 with a Blenheim from 139 Squadron flown by Flying Officer Alan MacLachlan, shot down near Bad Driburg. He added five more victims during the Battle of France before his first victory in the Battle of Britain with 8./JG 27 (formerly 2./JG 1): a Hurricane on 19 July 1940. In subsequent operations over France, the Channel and England he added further to a score that stood at 24[132] when he took off early that September morning.

By the time Adolph arrived in the Ostend–Blankenberge area it was already too late. The damage had been done. The Blenheims were on their way back home and 41 Squadron's Spitfires, operating in sections now, were simply looking for targets of opportunity. What followed was described in the squadron ORB as 'a running fight' between the two adversaries. It began for Babbage and his No 2, Pilot Officer Colin Jarred, when they engaged the incoming Fw 190s, albeit the new fighters were misidentified. As one of them made an ineffective firing pass at his No. 2, Babbage was mildly confused by the unfamiliar outline. It was certainly German. The black and white crosses on the fuselage were unmistakeable as it flashed past beneath him; but it wasn't the Me 109 he was accustomed to seeing. He couldn't be sure, but it looked a bit like a Curtiss 75A (he later described it as a Curtiss Hawk). Could the Luftwaffe have begun operating a few they acquired after the fall of France? But even that didn't really make sense. The aircraft he was now chasing as it headed back towards France after disengaging had a thinner fuselage. What surprised him, if it really was a Curtiss, was its performance – vastly superior to what he knew of the American-built aircraft.

All this was going through his mind as he tried to coax every ounce of speed from his Spitfire. He was almost flat out on the deck yet barely catching an enemy he thought must be short of either fuel or ammunition. Why else disengage after a single ineffective pass? Unless, of course, he'd lost his own wingman and was concerned about being outnumbered. Whatever the reason, it mattered not because, thankfully, the pilot didn't seem to be aware he was being stalked by two Spitfires, fast running out of fuel themselves. The coastline at Ostend loomed ever closer as Babbage finally came into range, dead astern his prey. A five-second burst, cannons and machine guns, and the mystery Luftwaffe fighter literally broke apart in front of him, large pieces crashing into the sea. With his fuel now dangerously low, it was time to head back to base and report not just his seventh confirmed – Jarred had witnessed the whole chase – but to start unravelling the mystery of his victim's identity. That would take time. Meanwhile Adolph's body was eventually washed ashore near Knokke in Belgium on 12 October. He was later buried in the German war cemetery at Lommel.

To help identify this new German aircraft, Babbage provided inputs to a contemporaneous sketch – a side elevation – that in the circumstances proved remarkably accurate. This says a good deal about him. One of the most important measures of a pilot's ability is spare capacity – being able to cope with the situation in hand whilst dealing with additional pressures in the shape of the unexpected. It's testament to Babbage's capabilities that during a life-or-death combat engagement, where he's conscious of his responsibility for his No. 2 as well, he's able to recognise the key features of an aircraft he's never met before. It was pilots like young Cyril Babbage, now aged just 24, who provided the first aid to recognition of an aircraft that was destined to hold sway over the RAF for nearly a year – until the Spitfire Mk IX was introduced in late July 1942. That said, even with its new Merlin engine and two-stage supercharger, this latest version would only match – and certainly not surpass – the Fw 190's performance. In the interim, the *Würger* (shrike or 'butcher bird') as it was known, was causing increasing concern. The RAF was desperate to get its hands on an example to uncover its secrets. But it wasn't until 23 June 1942 that its experts were able to examine the real thing – thanks to a disorientated German pilot who landed by mistake at RAF Pembrey, in South Wales. It's a story in itself.

The pilot concerned, Oberleutnant Armin Faber, normally mixed administrative duties with flying and needed special permission to fly a Fw 190 combat mission that day. He was part of a formation scrambled from Morlaix to intercept six Bostons from 107 Squadron as they returned from a bombing mission, escorted by Spitfires from the Perranporth and Exeter Wings. In the dogfight that subsequently developed over the Channel, Faber became separated from his colleagues and was attacked by a lone Spitfire. His efforts to shake it off led him north over Exeter where he finally managed to shoot down Sergeant Frantisek Trejtnar[133] of 310 (Czechoslovak) Squadron. The desperate manoeuvring necessary to avoid becoming a victim himself, let alone dispose of his opponent in a head-on attack, left Faber disorientated – so much so that he mistook the Bristol Channel for the English Channel and flew north instead of south. For him, South Wales became France, and spying a nearby airfield, he performed a victory roll celebration before setting himself up for a landing. Marshalled to the dispersal area of the training station that was Pembrey, the unknowing and soon desperately despondent Faber was promptly taken prisoner.

This stroke of good luck avoided the possible launch of an operation that had the potential to be seen as an audacious triumph or, more likely, a futile gesture. Reflecting the RAF's thirst for knowledge and the army's appetite for action, a daring plan to steal one of these new German fighters was being hatched. Operation Airthief was the brainchild of a commando officer, Captain Philip Pinckney.[134] He proposed that a friend, test pilot Jeffrey Quill,[135] should accompany him to bring back just such an aircraft from under the very noses of the Luftwaffe. He summarised his proposal to his CO thus:

To: Officer Commanding No.12 Commando
From: Captain Pinckney, E Troop, No. 12 Commando

Sir,

I understand that as a matter of great urgency and importance a specimen Focke-Wulf 190 is required in this country. I attach a proposal for procuring one of these aircraft.

I have the honour to request that this, my application to be allowed to undertake the operation described, may be forwarded as rapidly as possible through the correct channels to the Chief of Combined Operations. I further propose that the pilot to accompany me should be

Mr. Jeffrey Quill who is a close friend of mine, and as a well-known test pilot of fighter aircraft he is well qualified to bring back the plane. He is also young, active, a yachtsman, and a man in every way suitable to carry out the preliminary approach by land and sea.

If Mr. Quill cannot be allowed to undertake this operation, then perhaps a substitute could be made available from the Free French Forces? I am most anxious to be allowed to volunteer for this operation.

I have the honour to be, Sir,
Your obedient servant,

(signed) P. H. Pinckney

When it became clear there was no longer any imperative for such an operation, Quill was far from disappointed. He had doubts about his ability to fulfil his part of the bargain – unlike the plan's adventuresome instigator, in Quill's words, "a man of rare and timeless character'.[136] To him Pinckney was one of those who "appear from time to time in all ages, and seem set aside a little from their fellow men whether in peace or in war".[137] While Quill found himself carried along with his friend's enthusiasm, there were elements of the plan that concerned him, not least how Pinckney himself planned to get home if they were successful. Reflecting later on his own part in the operation:

"After a lot of thought and imagination I had concluded that, if I reached the cockpit of an aeroplane with the engine running, and provided the grass surfaces of the airfield were reasonable (they would be most carefully conned through powerful field glasses in advance) I had a 50-50 chance of getting back to an English airfield. As to the chances of ever reaching the cockpit I was not qualified to judge, but Philip was supremely confident . . ."[138]

By a remarkable coincidence, Pinckney's detailed plan was delivered to Combined Operations Headquarters on the very day, 23 June 1942, that

Faber landed his Fw 190 at Pembrey. When Pinckney learned of this, he was utterly dismayed and drove immediately to Eastleigh aerodrome on his army motorbike to give his friend the news. Quill, however, heaved a metaphorical sigh of relief and hoped "his sense of craven relief was not too apparent. There is no doubt that Philip was genuinely annoyed about the apparent sabotage of his much prized plan".[139]

Pinckney would lose his life in Italy some 15 months later. Dropped behind enemy lines on 6 September 1943 as part of a Special Air Service (SAS) operation, he was captured and executed next day under Hitler's infamous Commando Order.[140] Sad though he was when he heard the news, Quill was far from surprised. He'd earlier gained the impression that Philip could not survive the war and learned subsequently that he "was not alone in this belief. Philip also believed that he would not".[141] Pinckney was one of those mildly eccentric enthusiasts Britain regularly produces. Educated at Eton, he left Trinity College Cambridge after a year, travelled to India and then joined the family tea business. In a way he was "the least military-minded person imaginable",[142] but he "somehow transformed himself into a commando officer of repute", training others as small-boat raiders. It was this skill he planned to employ in delivering Quill to the shoreline once dropped from a naval motor gunboat. Notwithstanding his idiosyncrasies, he was held in high regard by those he commanded.[143] A leader of men can ask for little more.

Returning to the events of 18 September, while 41 Squadron had achieved much on their first operation of the day, the roadsted itself did not go according to plan. The same was true of Babbage's second sortie on an eventful day. He was part of an eight-aircraft contribution to Circus 97. The Tangmere Wing was to escort a raid by six Hampdens on the marshalling yards at Abbeville. However, the morning's fine weather had been replaced by afternoon cloud and fog over the Channel. This caused rendezvous problems for part of the escort package, squadrons from Debden and Hornchurch, problems exacerbated by confusion with another circus: a squadron of Blenheims heading for Rouen power station. The result was a recall for 41, first to Dungeness and then to base. Frustrating though it was for all concerned, such failures highlighted the difficulty of managing these complex packages.

While Babbage would fly no more operations during September, there was plenty of activity on the squadron, some of it unusual. The regular influx of the young and inexperienced continued on 19 September when four sergeants, two of them RCAF, were posted in. A circus operation the next day saw Flight Lieutenant Bache claim a half share in an Me 109E that was destroyed. There were more claims on 21 September: three damaged Me 109Es credited to Flight Lieutenant Charles Bush, Pilot Officer Ranger and Sergeant Whiteford. Bush had been posted in as OC A Flight a month before and was one of two flight commanders leading the squadron's offensive sweeps that day. Curiously, there was no Elmer Gaunce. For reasons unknown, the man who'd been appointed CO only six weeks earlier was posted to Tangmere with immediate effect. Not only that, his replacement arrived the very same day, Squadron Leader 'Dickie' Abrahams[144] from 91 Squadron at Hawkinge – 100 miles or so along the coast in Kent. To add to the mystery, Gaunce was back in post exactly a week later, marking his return by leading the first convoy patrol of the morning on 28 September. Meanwhile Abrahams, who flew not a single operational sortie during the interregnum (albeit there were remarkably few), was posted to 129 Squadron at Tangmere. What lay behind this strange set of circumstances remains frustratingly 'unclear'.[145] Speculation was no doubt rife, which would have done little for morale on a fighting unit where trust was what bound people together.

This unexplained hiatus apart, the month drew to a quiet close with limited convoy patrols, sweeps and a rhubarb – plus a few important announcements on 30 September: DFCs for Flight Lieutenant Marples, Flight Lieutenant Bush and Pilot Officer Bob Beardsley, together with the previously mentioned, richly deserved DFM for Sergeant Palmer.

The postings merry-go-round continued with Marples leaving after just over seven weeks on the squadron. His replacement as OC B Flight, Flight Lieutenant 'Bobby' Oxspring, arrived next day, 1 October, and immediately took part in an offensive sweep in company with Tangmere's 129 and 616 Squadrons, each providing eight aircraft. The 41 Squadron element, led by the CO, broke up off the French coast when attacked from above and behind by a number of Me 109Es. Fortunate to escape with no losses, the formation returned in dribs and drabs with Sergeant Whiteford claiming a damaged Me 109F.

Babbage flew with Oxspring next day, the latter's not untypical introduction to circus operations. Thanks to bad weather, things went wrong from the outset. The Tangmere Wing was unable to join up with the six Blenheims scheduled to attack Le Havre power station. All was not lost though. Diversionary sweeps by the North Weald, Hornchurch and Biggin Hill Wings became the main element of Circus 104, albeit at a cost: three pilots killed and a fourth wounded in return for five Me 109s destroyed and a sixth damaged. Later that same evening Babbage flew with his new flight commander again on another one-hour 30-minute sweep, this time with the Kenley Wing, but nothing came of it.

There followed a lull in operations – a week or so with no squadron-level sweeps, just a few convoy patrols and the odd rhubarb. AOC 11 Group, Air Vice-Marshal Trafford Leigh-Mallory, took the opportunity to visit Tangmere on 5 October. (He'd replaced Keith Park less than a month after the end of the Battle of Britain.) Then five days later the RAF's Inspector-General, Air Chief Marshal Sir Edgar Ludlow-Hewitt arrived at Merston to look at the site's facilities: dispersed dormitories, officers' sleeping quarters and the like.

It was a quiet period for Babbage too: just a short, one-hour sweep as part of a pair on 10 October. Things returned to near normal for him with a longer one-hour 30-minute offensive sweep two days later with the Tangmere Wing, where 65 Squadron had replaced 616, the latter moving to Kirton in Lindsey. Circus 107 was a major operation: 19 fighter squadrons supporting a raid by 24 Blenheims on Boulogne docks, albeit 41 Squadron's contribution was negligible. Part of the rear support wing, tasked with patrolling five miles off the French coast between Cap Gris-Nez and Boulogne, 12 Spitfires returned with nothing to report. By contrast, there was plenty to say the following day after the Wing's target support role in an attack on the St Omer shiplift by six Blenheims. Babbage would miss this; he was due eight days' leave. However, approval would be delayed until relatively late in the day – once the outcome of the afternoon sweep had been taken into account. Which was how he learned the chastening outcome of Circus 108A.

The squadron's problems began in the St Omer region when small formations of Me 109s appeared from all directions. A dozen Spitfires dissolved into smaller sections, and sections became individuals. One of these was the newly commissioned (as of 7 October) Pilot Officer George Swanwick, who claimed a damaged Me 109. Another who found himself alone was Pilot Officer Jarred. Near the coast, between Boulogne and Cap Gris-Nez, he lost contact with his section leader, Flight Lieutenant Leslie Bache, after they found themselves in company with a large number of enemy aircraft, mainly Fw 190s. Bache was reported lost. It would soon emerge that he'd been killed – likewise Sergeant Cyril Whiteford, last seen chasing after a badly damaged Me 109 in a near vertical dive. The CO, Elmer Gaunce, was the last to see him and submitted a claim for a probable on his behalf.

By way of a postscript to a sad day, the contrasting backgrounds of this unfortunate pair, who had joined the squadron within two days of each other at the end of August, make interesting reading. They reveal a stark imbalance between age, rank and experience. One, a 22-year-old sergeant, began his operational career six months earlier on 266 (Rhodesia) Squadron; he had a confirmed and a third share in another, the aforementioned probable, plus two damaged enemy aircraft to his credit. The other, a 28-year-old flight lieutenant, had barely seven weeks of operational experience, with just a half share in a single destroyed aircraft to his name. The contrast evident here illustrates just one of the many issues with which a CO had to grapple in protecting as best he could those under his command.

When Babbage finally left Merston next morning, little did he know he'd already flown his last sortie with 41 Squadron. During his absence, a posting notice arrived. Sadly, it meant there would be no opportunity for this 'very solid, keen and promising officer . . . an experienced section and flight leader' to take up the flight commander appointment for which he'd been recommended by his CO, Elmer Gaunce. Babbage's career was about to change direction. As of 18 October, he was posted to the RAF's Central Flying School (CFS) at Upavon.

CHAPTER 13

FAREWELL TO ARMS

The RAF has long prided itself on the quality of its flying instruction, and justifiably so. The process was formalised with the establishment of CFS at Upavon on 12 May 1912. There it remained until October 1926, when it relocated to Wittering. Nine years later, in August 1935, what remains the longest existing school for training military flying instructors returned to its birthplace.

The RAF's approach to instruction, mirrored later by air forces the world over, was based on a system developed by Robert Smith-Barry. A major in the RFC at the time, he'd seen his share of accidents. Shortly after the outbreak of World War I, on 14 August 1914 flying with 5 Squadron in France, he broke both legs when his B.E.8 crashed after the engine failed; the other occupant was killed.

Smith-Barry went on to serve at the RFC School of Special Flying at Gosport. Here in December 1916, he introduced a curriculum that proved the model for what followed. 'The Gosport System', as it later became known, fused the classroom and the cockpit – academic training plus dual instruction. But the key to its success was the underpinning philosophy. Rather than avoiding potentially dangerous manoeuvres, which had been the approach until then, instructors now deliberately took students to the edges of the flying envelope in a controlled environment, thus enabling them to recognise and recover from potentially hazardous situations. Smith-Barry's approach proved a masterstroke. It would underpin Babbage's own approach to flying for the next two-and-a-half years – longer than his flying career thus far.

Up until this point, Babbage had given no thought to what might lay beyond the immediacy of day-to-day survival in his Spitfire. How would he cope with teaching another individual how to fly? He wasn't sure. He remembered all too well his own faltering first steps en route to the award of the coveted flying badge: the wings that meant so much to him and his fellow NCOs. It was hard to believe that it was less than two years ago. So much had happened in the interim. Back then the instructors had seemed omnipotent. A self-effacing individual who shunned the limelight, Babbage felt any transformation to this God-like status would be, at the very least, unlikely. That said, it was hard to deny that his operational experiences of the last 18 months or so had brought a new confidence, a justified belief in his own ability. And he was determined to succeed.

Babbage's short CFS course began on 22 October 1941. Just over seven weeks later, on 12 December, four days after his promotion, Flying Officer Cyril Babbage graduated as a B2 instructor on single-engined aircraft. In a system that remains to this day, CFS instructors were graded A1, A2, B1 and B2, the last named being the norm on completion of the CFS course. Advancement to higher grades came with experience and appropriate levels of testing both in the air and on the ground.

His first posting was to No. 9 FTS, Hullavington, on 14 December. Notwithstanding the vagaries of the English winter, he was soon exceptionally busy – busy enjoying himself too. February 1942 would prove the first of several challenging months: more than 50 hours' flying, including ten at night and nearly seven in the Hurricane. While Babbage was learning fast, a minor accident that same month demonstrated the perils associated with teaching the inexperienced. On 11 February he was flying a Miles Master with a student in the front seat when the aircraft was damaged landing at Castle Combe, then a relief landing ground for Hullavington. The damage was only minor (described as 'repairable'), caused by lack of a tailwheel. It had fallen off – almost certainly the result of poor landing technique on the student's part. That such an incident should occur so early in Babbage's instructing career is by no means unusual. He'd yet to witness anything like the full spectrum of difficulties an inexperienced student could encounter.

At the time, Castle Combe was also home to No. 7 Flying Instructors School (FIS), where Fleet Air Arm pilots trained on the Albacore and Swordfish – two of the more unusual types Babbage soon added to his logbook. In the summer of 1942 what would soon become a peripatetic instructing career took him back to Upavon and No. 7 FIS (as CFS had been renamed) for just over two months. Then, on 1 August he moved to 3 FIS, first at Castle Combe and then Lulsgate Bottom. It was there, a year to the day after his previous promotion, and now a B1 instructor, that on 8 December 1942 he added a second stripe to his uniform; he was now a flight lieutenant. A year almost to the day after his promotion, on 12 December 1943 Babbage returned to Upavon for a significant upgrade: from B1 instructor to A2 (multi-engined) category. Little did he realise this was the prelude to his next appointment.

On 29 March 1944 he was posted to No. 1482 Bombing & Gunnery Flight at Swanton Morley, near Norwich. The unit title tells only part of the story here. As well as providing target-towing and gunnery practice, it supplied replacement aircraft and crews for 2 Group's squadrons during and after the D-Day landings in France. This is where Babbage's Record of Service introduces the first of a series of confusing contradictions. Official records indicate that 1482 Flight was disbanded on 1 April 1944.[146] But it was indeed at Swanton Morley that Babbage qualified on the Mosquito, flying his first crew 'solo' on 7 April. While an OTU Mosquito course normally lasted some eight weeks, as a highly experienced pilot with over 2,000 hours in his logbook and experience on a variety of aircraft types,[147] Babbage completed a short, tailored conversion course designed to speed his progress to the front line. He was destined for a night intruder squadron.

CHAPTER 14

THE NIGHT INTRUDER

Almost a month after his posting to Swanton Morley, on 28 April 1944 Babbage arrived at Gravesend to join 464 Squadron Royal Australian Air Force (RAAF). More than two-and-a-half years after leaving the front line, he was back there again.

So much had changed since he left 41 Squadron at Merston. But he was hardly aware. He'd been insulated from the harsh realities of war in a different environment, displaced not just physically but psychologically too. No longer was the aim simply to survive – to get through the next sortie in one piece. The mark of success in the flying training world lay less in his own achievements, more in those of others – guiding his students through their inevitable difficulties, seeing them safely to the moment when they could pin on the precious RAF flying badge. En route to that coming of age as a pilot, he shared with them the struggle, the frustrations, the enjoyment, the wonder and the sheer beauty of flying. Instructing wasn't a job where he could ever really relax though. Even the best students had the capacity to surprise the unwary or complacent instructor. But for Babbage, flying never lost its romance; the landscapes he looked down on never lost their allure. And there was an almost sensual pleasure in being alone in the sky – even when it was 'alone' with a student.

Meanwhile, the front line had benefited from some of the changes in the training world that Babbage witnessed. Latterly he'd been part of a system that delivered better qualified aircrew – pilots with more hours than before – to the OTUs, and thence to the squadrons, than had been the case in his day. Those arriving on operational units now were generally more experienced than previously. The nature of the RAF's war had also changed: from the post-Battle of Britain fighter operations in which he'd played a part, to Bomber Command's strategic offensive. In this latter context the RAF now had help in the shape of the US Eighth Air Force in taking the battle to the enemy – and with a vengeance. Not just in the shape of increasingly accurate bombing, but with fighter cover from the P-51 Mustang all the way to the most distant targets and back again. Indeed, the Eighth Air Force made a major contribution to achieving the air supremacy without which the D-Day landings could not have taken place.

If the Mustang was an American success story, there were three equally outstanding British aircraft during World War II.[148] Babbage may well have been unique in flying all three of these – the Mustang too.[149] He had already proved himself on the Spitfire when, in mid-August 1943, he had a brief opportunity to fly the Lancaster at No. 1662 Heavy Conversion Unit,[150] RAF Blyton, in Lincolnshire. Soon he would have his mettle tested on the third of this trio, the Mosquito – and at a critical time. D-Day was in the offing. To put the challenge Babbage now faced into context, it was a function of three factors: a new aircraft, a new squadron and a new role.

The DH 98 Mosquito, later known as 'the Wooden Wonder', began life with a less flattering soubriquet: 'Freeman's Folly'. This was thanks to Lord Beaverbrook, the man Churchill appointed as Minister for Aircraft Production in early May 1940. It referenced Air Chief Marshal Sir Wilfrid Freeman,[151] without whose support Geoffrey de Havilland's[152] wooden aircraft design might never have seen the light of day. After the fall of France, Beaverbrook told Freeman that work on the prototype should stop. He was concerned that it might absorb resources better devoted to other projects critical to the country's defence. Freeman simply refused – on the grounds that he was issued no specific instructions to cancel the project. That said, lack of materials did cause a temporary halt in production of the prototype; but the project was reinstated after de Havilland's general manager[153] promised Beaverbrook delivery of 50 aircraft by December 1941. In the event the target was missed, but only by three months. The gamble was worth it.

What lay behind de Havilland's belief in wooden construction? A far-sighted individual, for some time he'd seen war with Germany as inevitable. And when, not if, war came, there would be shortages of aluminium and steel. He therefore needed to consider alternative resources. Wood products would not only be more readily available, they also had advantages, not least a strength-to-weight ratio equal to or better than light alloys or steel (albeit they were less good under tension). Geoffrey de Havilland's faith in what was effectively a radical departure for a modern aircraft paved the way for a remarkable success. The immensely capable and versatile twin-engined Mosquito went on to fill a variety of roles, including night fighter, fighter-bomber, medium bomber, photo reconnaissance and anti-shipping. Of 7,781 aircraft eventually produced, 6,710 were built during the war; 1,076 were manufactured in Canada and 212 in Australia.

The version Babbage was destined to operate was the Mosquito FB Mk VI fighter-bomber designed for 'intruder' strike missions, the most numerous and widely used Mosquito variant. Based on the F Mk II day-fighter version, less its air interception radar, it retained the formidable armament of four Browning .303 machine guns in the nose and four Hispano 20mm cannon in the belly. Behind these a bomb bay was added which carried two 500lb bombs; two more could be attached under the wings. Designed to operate primarily at low altitude, it was unpressurised and retained single-stage supercharged Merlin engines.

Few examples of the aircraft's use better illustrate its capability, or indeed 464 Squadron's place within an elite force, than a daring, low-level bombing raid carried out two months or so before Babbage arrived: Operation Jericho, the attack on Amiens prison on 18 February 1944. Purportedly triggered by news that 12 members of the Resistance held there would be executed the following day, it was carried out by the three squadrons of No. 140 Wing, 2nd Tactical Air Force (2TAF), supported by Typhoons from 174 and 198 Squadrons. The meticulously planned and precisely timed raid – the Germans were expected to be at lunch – was to comprise three six-aircraft waves with OC 140 Wing, Group Captain P.C. 'Pick' Pickard,[154] in overall command and flying the sixth 464 Squadron aircraft.

Appalling UK weather created problems from the outset. Four Mosquitos lost contact with the rest of their formations and a fifth returned with an engine fire. This meant that only five aircraft from 487 Squadron Royal New Zealand Air Force (RNZAF) arrived at 1201, tasked with breaching two sections of the prison outer wall – not easy, given it was some 20ft high and 3ft thick. The second wave, from 464 Squadron, was down to just four aircraft when it arrived. Too close behind, with smoke and debris partially obscuring the target, they had to circle the prison once before attacking. With the eastern wall apparently undamaged, one pair bombed the wall from 50ft. The remaining two Mosquitos successfully targeted the main building, bombing from 100ft. Seeing prisoners escaping while he orbited at low level, Group Captain Pickard then cleared 21 Squadron's third wave to return home. Held in reserve pending results from the first two attacks, their remaining four aircraft weren't needed.

The man who would be Babbage's first CO when he arrived on 464, Wing Commander Bob Iredale,[155] recalled the attack:

> "I pinpointed the guards' quarters, let go my bombs so that they would skid right into the annexe, then pulled up into a steep climb. It was all over as quickly as that, with the sloping roof of the prison inches from the belly of my plane as I climbed over it. Back behind me my bombs exploded.[156] The building housing the German guards seemed to shudder and disintegrate."[157]

Bold and precise though it was, the raid could be seen as only a mixed success. Of more than 700 prisoners, 102 were killed and 74 wounded – either during the attack or by the Germans. A total of 258 escaped, including half of those due to be shot, 79 of whom were either Resistance workers or political prisoners; 182 of the escapees were later recaptured. Set against these statistics, and a degree of mystery that remains to this day over the tasking, must be the loss of two 464 Squadron Mosquitos and three of their four aircrew. Group Captain Pickard and his navigator, Flight Lieutenant 'Bill' Broadley,[158] were shot down by a Fw 190 and killed. This was almost certainly the result of spending too long orbiting the target area. Pickard even cleared 21 Squadron to return home when the responsibility for this decision lay with the photo-reconnaissance Mosquito following up the attack.

Given the proximity of the Luftwaffe fighter base at Abbeville, barely 25 miles away, and notwithstanding the presence of supporting Typhoons, the Mosquitos were always at risk from interception. The single 464 Squadron individual who survived, Squadron Leader Ian McRitchie, was badly injured by the same heavy groundfire that killed his navigator, Flight Lieutenant R.W. Sampson. He somehow managed to crash land his flak-damaged aircraft near Amiens before passing out; he spent the rest of the war imprisoned. Two of the escorting Typhoons from 174 Squadron were also lost, as was one of the pilots, Flight Sergeant H.S. Brown, last seen flying into a snow cloud over the Channel. The other, Flying Officer J.E. Reynaud, was taken prisoner after being shot down north of Amiens.

Turning now to 464 Squadron itself, what was behind the establishment of the RAAF unit that now lay claim to Babbage's loyalty? It was one of eight such Bomber Command units known as 'article XV squadrons'. The article in question related to the agreement under which the Empire Air Training Scheme (EATS) was established early in the war, when it became clear that the RAF would be unable to produce enough pilots to meet its needs. The governing EATS agreement provided training for nearly 50,000 aircrew each year: 22,000 from Britain, 13,000 from Canada, 11,000 from Australia and 3,300 from New Zealand. Crews would receive elementary training in their home country while Canada would provide advanced courses. Article XV of the agreement stipulated that graduates serving with the RAF should be placed in new squadrons identified with their country of birth, i.e. as RAAF, RCAF and RNZAF units, albeit under RAF operational control. In practice, most of these individuals were assigned to RAF units, certainly initially. Eventually, however, Australia boasted 17 article XV squadrons. Formed in August 1942, the following June 464 Squadron was transferred from Bomber Command to 2TAF as part of No. 140 Wing, No. 2 Group – a move reflecting the group's new, offensive role in direct support of the army. Initially equipped with Venturas, 464 completed its conversion to Mosquitos as a night intruder in September 1943.

The change in 2 Group's role made sense in the context of the war as a whole. Its aircraft had been involved in offensive operations since Babbage's time with 41 Squadron. The circuses in which he'd taken part, designed to lure Luftwaffe fighters into the air, used 2 Group aircraft as bait for Fighter Command's trap. When Babbage joined 464 changes were afoot within Bomber Command too. Its formidable Commander-in-Chief, Air Chief Marshal Sir Arthur 'Bomber' Harris,[159] had just been forced to embrace the requirements of Operation Overlord, specifically the 'Transportation Plan'. The brainchild of Professor 'Solly' Zuckerman,[160] regarded as one of the best minds in operational research, this was a strategic bombing offensive against bridges, road and rail junctions, marshalling yards and repair facilities in France. The aim was to isolate the battlefield, to hamper enemy troop movements and render reinforcement of the invasion area as difficult as possible. The approach was entirely consistent with views expressed by Montgomery[161] as early as 10 January. To protect the proposed invasion, from D-Day to D plus 14 he needed the French railways out of commission at a radius of 150 miles from the invasion point.[162]

Initially Harris was prepared to offer only relatively short-range aircraft, Stirlings and Halifaxes, for preparatory attacks on France. Arguing that his Lancaster squadrons would be less effective against smaller, pinpoint targets allowed him to retain them for the strategic offensive he was convinced would soon bring Germany to its knees. General Carl 'Tooey' Spaatz, commander of the US Eighth Air Force, was similarly reluctant to prejudice his own objectives, where attacks on oil refineries and German fighter production were proving similarly effective. Moreover, both commanders were reluctant to see their forces placed under the control of General Eisenhower,[163] Supreme Commander of the Allied Expeditionary Force (AEF). It was not until the last two months before the invasion that a difficult situation was resolved – not a moment too soon, and not without a degree of acrimony. Relationships at the highest levels of command deteriorated as Eisenhower insisted that the direction of all Allied air forces must be subordinated to him. Sharing Harris's concerns, Churchill was particularly exercised over the possibility of significant French civilian casualties. He felt this could leave their anticipated liberators, the British and the Americans, facing 'a legacy of hate' that would forever besmirch air forces' reputations. In the end, and only after the intervention of President Roosevelt,[164] both had to concede the primacy of Operation Overlord – preparations for which effectively set the template for Babbage's first few weeks with his new squadron.

The transportation plan also formed part of the D-Day deception plan. In April and May Allied bombing raids had been much heavier in the Calais area, certainly in comparison with the real landing sites. This effort across northern France to hamper the means by which Axis forces could reinforce Normandy succeeded beyond expectations. Some 1,500 of the 2,000 railway engines in the Nord département were immobilised, helping to confirm in the enemy's mind that the anticipated attack would come from the Pas-de-Calais. It was a plan in which 464 Squadron would play a significant part.

If the success of the Normandy invasion owed everything to preparation, planning and deception, it would have been impossible without first achieving air supremacy. A concerted Allied effort during the early months of 1944 had drastically reduced the Luftwaffe's effectiveness: 'between January and April the day-fighter force had lost over 1,000 pilots, including some of the best commanders'.[165] However, the extent of the Allies' success in this respect was not fully appreciated until D-Day itself. There remained concerns that the Germans might still be able to muster substantial numbers of both fighters and bombers in a single effort over Normandy on the day. According to some historians, on 6 June the Luftwaffe could muster only a paltry 319 sorties.[166] Another suggests that they 'put less than a hundred fighters into the sky on D-Day and mounted only 22 sorties against shipping late that evening'.[167] Such statistics are not necessarily inconsistent, and whatever the truth, there can be no doubt that command of the air on 6 June was fundamental to the success of the Normandy landings.

When Babbage had joined his new squadron a few short weeks earlier, 464 was based at Gravesend in Kent. Originally 'a postage stamp' of an airfield and the bane of Spitfire pilots' lives – the runway was barely long enough for fully armed aircraft, resulting in regular crashes – it lay close to the south bank of the Thames. But by April 1944 it had been expanded to accommodate the three Mosquito squadrons of No. 140 Wing. That said, 464 Squadron's arrival there on 17 April had echoes of the airfield's past. One aircraft crashed on landing, although the crew were unhurt. Next morning another crashed on take-off with the same result. Hearing of this after he arrived brought back uncomfortable thoughts of Babbage's early days at Drem and the problems those new to the Spitfire encountered there. New to the Mosquito he might be, but he boasted a wealth of experience – experience gained the hard way – that would stand him in good stead.

Shortly after he settled in, on 30 April the base hosted a visit by AOC No. 2 Group, Air Vice-Marshal Basil Embry.[168] The day was marked by an official parade and march past, which struck Babbage as somewhat incongruous. But then he'd been away from the front line for some time. Maybe this was the norm now – a balance between wartime operations overseas and something approaching peacetime formality at home. Putting such thoughts aside, he had to acknowledge the respect this brave, pugnacious and outspoken visitor commanded amongst his fellow airmen. Embry was unusual in that even as an air vice-marshal he flew on operations. In fact, he'd intended to lead the Amiens prison raid, flying with the man who'd played a key role in planning the attack, Flight Lieutenant 'Ted' Sismore.[169] However, Air Marshal Sir Arthur Coningham,[170] Commander-in-Chief (C-in-C) 2TAF, ordered him not to take part on the grounds that he knew too much about the background to the raid, and indeed the Normandy invasion itself. His capture would therefore be potentially prejudicial. (Strangely, Embury then banned Sismore from taking part, much to the latter's frustration.) In an aside that will sound familiar to today's reader, 12 years later on Embry's 'retirement' aged only 53 from a service that had no further jobs or indeed room for him, *Time* magazine[171] summarised his views thus: 'the R.A.F. is unready for atomic war, dominated by the civil service, shackled to outdated strategy and outmoded jet types by pound-pinchers at Her Majesty's Treasury.'

The first signs of the role Cyril Babbage, Mosquito pilot, was to play in the D-Day preparations became evident shortly before he arrived. On 28 April the ORB records, 'A new venture – six aircraft to bomb a railway yard in northern France in conjunction with 6 a/c of 21 Squadron. All a/c were to be led by two Pathfinder aircraft of 8 Group.' The Master Bomber flew in a 109 Squadron Mosquito fitted with Oboe[172] blind-bombing equipment. Bomber Command may have graduated from massed area bombing to a force capable of precision targeting, but this particular raid went badly, with bombs falling seven miles from the target. Undeterred by failure, a similar approach was used for three subsequent raids on the same location, Abancourt railway yards: on 30 April, 1 May and 3 May. With cloud obscuring the target each time, results were unobserved but it was believed that bombs fell within 300 yards of the railway centre on at least one of these occasions. On 6 May the target changed to the V-1[173] site at Yvrench–Conteville; tactics remained the same but this time 464 provided only three of the 12 attacking aircraft.

This was the prelude to Babbage's first operational sortie on 9 May, the daylight bombing of a target in northern France. Crewed with Flying Officer N.E. McIntyre, his was one of six Mosquitos that took off in the early afternoon for a sortie of just over two hours. It proved a sobering introduction. Despite climbing to 20,000ft before crossing the Channel, and bombing from the same height, intense and accurate German flak damaged one aircraft. Unable to make it back to base, Flying Officer H.W. Tuck and his navigator, Pilot Officer A.D. Crowfoot, were forced to crash land at Bradwell Bay on the Essex coast, 30 miles north-east of Gravesend. When their aircraft overshot the runway they were both seriously injured and immediately taken to hospital.

If a single, relatively undemanding operational sortie was all Babbage had to show for his first month on 464 Squadron, he was gradually becoming more comfortable with his new aircraft, more adept too at using its formidable weapons. There was plenty of opportunity to practise strafing and dive-bombing ground targets, and indeed to develop the crew cooperation that would be so important in the months ahead. While he was frustrated at the lack of action, what little the squadron accomplished in operational terms for the rest of the month took place mainly at night: 40 of 54 sorties. And he needed to gain more experience in this respect too. The squadron's emphasis on night low-level interdiction would demand every ounce of ability he and McIntyre could muster as a crew.

Flying apart, two other events caught his attention towards the end of the month, albeit for different reasons. First, there was a formal church parade on

Sunday 28 May, which struck Babbage as slightly odd – a thought reflected in the related ORB entry: 'The band provided by A.T.C. [Air Training Corps] was appreciated. It seems that we must be devoid of singers as few appeared to join in the hymn singing.' Second, and more telling, were remarks the following day from Sir Arthur Coningham. Commenting on his visit, the ORB provides an insight into the preparations for D-Day. The squadron 'listened to an inspiring address in which [the C-in-C] indicated what our part is to be when "the big show" starts'. Appetites for action thus whetted, the sense of anticipation at Gravesend was almost tangible. But Babbage and his colleagues had a few days yet to wait.

Meanwhile, the final entry in the ORB for May offers testament to the effectiveness of Babbage's new aircraft. Summarising the activities of Squadron Leader Geoff Oxlade, OC A Flight, on the night of 31 May it reports thus: 'Several attacks made with cannon fire on MT [motor transport] convoys . . . with very good results – one vehicle blown to pieces and several other strikes observed.' Oxlade's sortie, one of a pair where the other pilot was OC 464 Squadron, Wing Commander Iredale, set the tone for what was to come. Babbage would not fly a single operational sortie by day throughout June. In fact, the squadron would be tasked with only three daylight missions during the entire month: a pair on a last-minute task towards the middle plus a reconnaissance sortie near the end of June. These aberrations apart, the emphasis was entirely on night-time support for the Normandy invasion. But the portents were less than encouraging. At 2255 on 2 June, the first of two three-aircraft waves set off across the Channel to carry out intruder raids into France, attacking trains, bridges and airfields. The second followed at 0015. Individual aircraft were separated by 10-/15-minute intervals, except for the final pair, which took off at the same time. Only one of them returned. It was an all-too-familiar tale. Flying Officers R.A. Faulafer and R.A. Wilkins, a crew on their first operation, were lost without trace.

Next day Babbage was intrigued by an apparent hive of activity – and this despite the lack of flying. At Gravesend, and at airfields all over England, aircraft were being painted with black and white identification stripes around the fuselage and on the upper and lower surfaces of the wings. Aircraft adorned with these 'D-Day stripes' were not allowed within 20 miles of the

Above left: Sergeant 'Ginger' Whall, 602 Squadron. (Andy Saunders Collection)

Above right: The ill-fated Sergeant Mervyn Sprague, 602 Squadron, killed four days after returning from honeymoon. (Andy Saunders Collection)

Right: Pilot Officer 'Pat' Lyall, 602 Squadron. (Andy Saunders Collection)

Below: Flight Lieutenant Dunlop Urie's short-lived 602 Squadron Spitfire, X4110. Newly delivered, it lacked 602 Squadron markings. (Andy Saunders Collection)

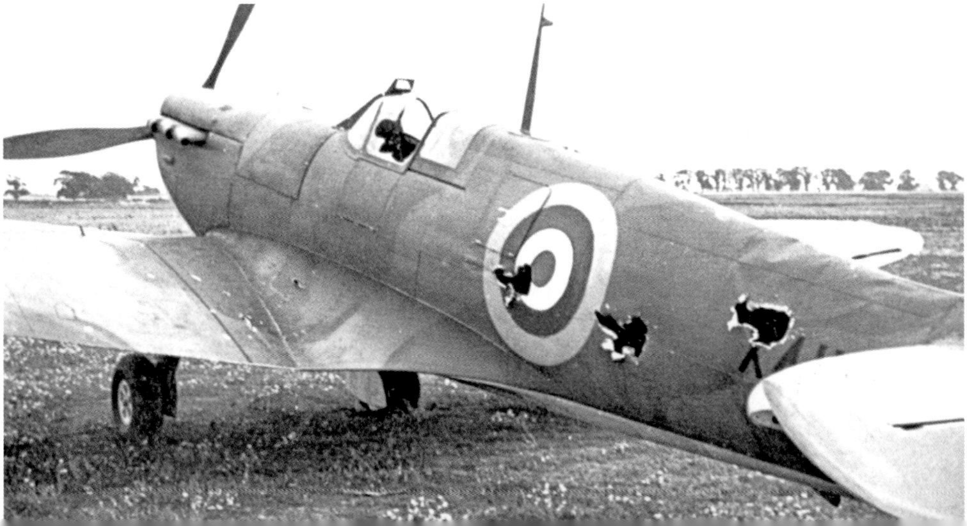

Above: The Ju 88 shot down by Pilot Officers Lyall and Hanbury, 602 Squadron, 21 September 1940, crash-landed near Bosham. (Andy Saunders Collection)

Above: Sergeant Babbage with his treasured MG. (Babbage family archive)

Below: Some of these Windmill girls attended Jack Boret's epic Tangmere party.

Above: Sir Patrick Dollan, Lord Provost of Glasow (centre), entertained 602 Squadron personnel to lunch, 8 March 1941. Babbage is second left, back row. (Francis Wells)

Right: Pilot Officer Babbage wearing his trademark scarf. (Francis Wells)

Below left: Squadron Leader Donald Finlay, OC 41 Squadron when Babbage arrived. (Swanwick family)

Below right: Sergeant Alan Bull who flew his early 41 Squadron operations with Babbage. (Nigel Aspdin)

Above: It's easy to see why Babbage likened the Curtiss Hawk to a Fw 190. (Steve Brew)

Below: Fw 190. (Steve Brew)

Bottom: The remarkably accurate scale drawing based on pilots' impressions of the Fw 190. (Chris Goss)

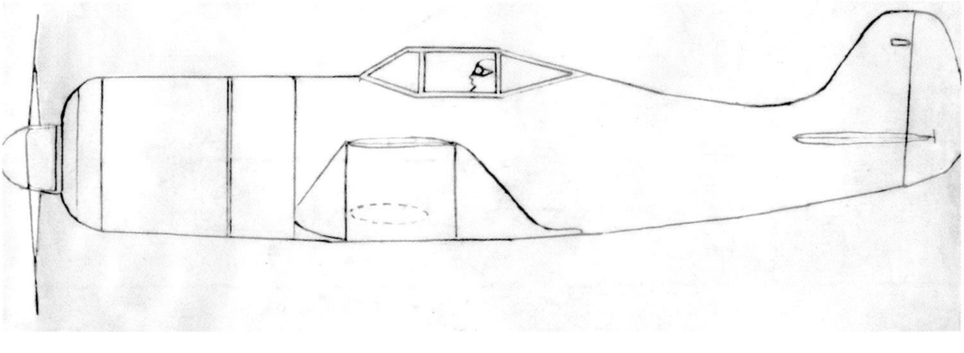

Above: Hauptmann Walter Adolph, seated centre, killed when Babbage shot down his Fw 190, 19 September 1941. (Chris Goss)

Below: No. 464 Squadron Mosquitos at Sculthorpe, October 1943. The tall figure is Group Captain 'Pick' Pickard. (de Havilland Aircraft Museum)

Below: Flight Lieutenant Babbage with his mother and sister, Betty, 1943 or later. Nothing more is known about what was clearly an important occasion. (Babbage family archive)

Above: No. 464 Squadron Mosquitos photographed by Babbage's navigator. (Babbage family archive)

Left: A 464 Squadron Mosquito in D-Day stripes. (Babbage family archive)

Below: Mosquitos could inflict fearsome damage. (Babbage family archive)

Above: John Tonkin, second left, the SAS commander who helped wreak havoc behind the German lines after D-Day.

Right: A plaque commemorating the raid on the Gestapo barracks at Bonneuil-Matours.

Below left: Squadron Leader and Mrs Babbage on their wedding day, 28 June 1945. (Babbage family archive)

Below right: Squadron Leader Babbage in tropical mess kit, taken during his time in Cyprus. (Francis Wells)

Left: Babbage instructed on the Vampire T.11 at Merryfield. (Babbage family archive)

Below: Wing Commander Babbage at D Unit. (Babbage family archive)

Below left: Wing Commander Cyril Babbage. (Babbage family archive)

Below right: Babbage's gravestone at Haycombe Cemetery, Bath.

Continent unless and until specifically tasked. There was now a heightened air of expectancy. Babbage could feel the excitement, the anticipation, as his new squadron was briefed for a maximum effort of 20 sorties on the night of 5/6 June. Targets would be road convoys, railway facilities and road junctions in northern France, all critical to the movement of enemy troops towards the invasion area. These operations were not without risk – and not just to the airmen of 464 Squadron. Echoing Churchill's earlier misgivings, collateral damage to the civilian population was a particular concern for Air Chief Marshal Sir Trafford Leigh-Mallory, C-in-C of the Allied Expeditionary Air Force, when he put forward his plan to interdict the routes enemy formations might use. But it was a risk that Eisenhower was prepared to take: an operational necessity. In any event, and despite the need to expand interdiction operations along the whole of the Channel coast and across northern France to disguise the real landing site, civilian casualties were less than Churchill had feared. But they were substantial, nevertheless. Prior to the invasion 15,000 French civilians were killed and 19,000 injured.[174]

As midnight approached on Monday 5 June, a massive air armada of over 1,200 aircraft was preparing to take off from airfields all over central and southern England. Three airborne divisions would soon be en route to the Normandy coast in Horsa gliders towed by Halifax bombers. Earlier that evening the largest fleet ever assembled began to leave Southampton Water. Channels to the French coast would be cleared by 277 minesweepers; some 5,000 landing ships and assault craft would follow, escorted by six battleships, four monitors (small warships with large guns), 23 cruisers, 104 destroyers and 152 escort vessels.[175]

Meanwhile at Gravesend, as the crews of 464 Squadron prepared to play their own part in the events of D-Day, the almost incessant sound of bombers passing overhead provided the first inkling of the sheer scale of the operation in which they were about to take part. The first wave of 16 Mosquitos set off for their targets in France at regular intervals between 2200 and 2345. Babbage and McIntyre were fourth in the stream and took off at 2220 for a two-hour sortie. A second wave of four aircraft launched in similar fashion from 0300. Babbage's target was the railway line that ran south out of Brionne. The town itself was some 50 miles due east of Caen, which would become the site of fierce fighting in the days and weeks ahead as the Allies struggled to break out from the beachhead. Frustratingly, like so many attacks during the period of intensive operations that was to follow, the results of Babbage's efforts were 'not seen' (alternative ORB formulations were 'not known' or 'unobserved').

Sadly, one crew failed to return, Squadron Leader Oxlade and Flight Lieutenant Donald Shanks. Taking off half-an-hour later than Babbage, they were picked up by searchlights after coasting in and immediately targeted by several flak batteries. Unable to escape their attention, Oxlade's Mosquito was severely damaged and eventually the engines failed. With his aircraft now on fire, Oxlade ordered his navigator to bail out near Yvetot, some 20 miles north-west of Rouen. Unable to follow suit, he was killed in the subsequent crash. Shanks himself had a remarkable escape. After landing in an area full of German billets associated with nearby V-1 sites, he was fortunate to be found and hidden by French farmers. In doing so they placed their own lives at mortal risk. But thanks to their help, an individual known for his resilience remained at large in the same area for more than two months. Eventually, in late August, he was repatriated, thanks to the Allies' advance. Indicative of the bond that holds operational squadrons together, one of Shanks' first actions on returning to the UK was to find and then visit his erstwhile squadron, which had by then relocated.

The atmosphere at Gravesend next day was electric. Exhausted crews, four of whom had flown twice the previous night, sat glued to the radio listening to BBC reports of the Allied landings. By 1500 the invasion was apparently going 'satisfactorily'. But there would be no respite for the squadron that night. Eventually they flew 27 sorties against the same target sets as before: road and rail junctions plus enemy troop convoys. This time eight crews would fly twice. It was a long night. The first of the generally staggered take-offs came at 2225, with the start of the second wave at 0240 and last landing at 0655. In fact, it was daylight by the time the last four crews touched down. Babbage took off at 0030, patrolling and attacking roads in the Falaise area using target indicator flares. The principle was the same: block possible reinforcement routes for any enemy formations. With no longer any need to hide the invasion location, targets like Babbage's, to the south and south-west of Caen were favoured. This led to longer sorties than the previous night; many, like his, were around three hours.

As before, results were hard to judge, but the squadron recorded successes against at least two large vehicle convoys. Given that this time every aircraft returned safely, spirits on the squadron were high, aircrew and ground crew alike. After all, they'd just set a record for the number of sorties flown in a single night, beating that set the previous evening by 21 Squadron. Despite being permitted to sleep in, ground crew were soon at work preparing the 15 aircraft required for another effort on the night of 7 June. They did so against the constant background of aircraft noise overhead – support en route to the Normandy beaches. Tasking and patrol locations were as before, to the south and south-west of Caen. The first take-off for the single wave required was at 2355, the last at 0050. Babbage took off on a two-hour 20-minute sortie at 0055. Not given to self-praise, he reported that the road/railway bridge he targeted was 'believed hit', but he couldn't be certain. Such caginess had become the norm; frustratingly, few crews were able to see positive results from their bombing attacks. Strafe attacks on the other hand were easier to assess, often through fires and secondary explosions. The only events to dampen spirits on this third night of operations were the return of one aircraft with a port engine failure and another with electrical problems that prevented bomb release. The safe return of all crews was always welcomed but never guaranteed.

There was no flying for Babbage on the next three days, one of which, 9 June, was lost due to bad weather. This interruption apart, the squadron was settling into a similar pattern of night sorties against convoys, road and rail junctions, trains and bridges in support of the Normandy landings. The norm was to transit the Channel at 5,000ft, then cross the French coast in a dive to around 3,000ft on dark nights and nearer 1,000ft when there was moonlight, descending lower for bombing or strafing. While 8 June was relatively quiet – 12 staggered take-offs from 2240 through to 0215 – two days later was anything but.

With the prospect of 27 night sorties on 10 June in the familiar two-wave pattern, crews first busied themselves with what the ORB refers to as NFTs – night flying tests. These were short daylight sorties of 20-30 minutes, flown to ensure all aircraft equipment, even the guns, functioned just as it should. While

NFTs were a reassuring precaution, they were no insurance against subsequent failures, as events would soon prove. The first aircraft took off at 2230 while the second wave, comprising five crews on their second sortie, began at 0200. But the night was marked by another loss: Captain 'Andy' Wakeman USAAF and his navigator, Flying Officer Geoffrey Holmes. Their aircraft took off at 0011 hours[176] but within minutes was seen crashing into the Thames, killing both occupants. The American's body was picked up from the river next day. The cause of this tragic accident was thought to be double engine failure just after take-off, placing the crew in a situation from which it was impossible to recover.

The next day, 11 June, was marked once again by the drone of heavy traffic overhead. It began in unpropitious fashion. After completing an NFT on the aircraft he was due to fly that evening, Flight Sergeant Glyn Williams crashed on landing in a strong crosswind. Neither he nor his navigator, Flight Sergeant John Dunn, were injured; indeed, they flew again the following night. But the damage was enough to trigger a request for an immediate replacement aircraft. Babbage was in one of 14 aircraft that set off for France later that evening. The first two of these took off in daylight at 2030, bound for a target 200 miles south of the Normandy beaches, at Châtellerault. It makes for an unusual story, albeit one with a sting in the tail – eventually.

Prior to D-Day Allied air superiority was such that the Germans found it almost impossible to move critical supplies, fuel and the like, across northern France. It was simply too great a risk. Their solution was to route materiel to Normandy from the south via Marseille. To hamper and disrupt the progress of these German reinforcements, a team from B Squadron 1st SAS was dropped behind enemy lines from 6 June onwards. This was Operation Bulbasket. Situated in an area to the east of Poitiers in south-west France, where it linked with fighters from the Maquis, the team's task was to destroy supply dumps, block the Paris to Bordeaux railway line near Poitiers and attack railway sidings and fuel trains. More specifically, it was to delay the arrival in Normandy of the 2nd SS[177] Panzer Division, *Das Reich*, from Toulouse – a journey of some 500 miles for its 15,000 men and 1,400 vehicles that began on 8 June.

Shortly after landing in France the SAS commander, Captain John Tonkin,[178] learned the whereabouts of a parked supply train, 20 rail cars of fuel reserves for the Panzers, in a siding near Châtellerault. When reconnaissance to confirm its exact location revealed it was too heavily guarded to risk an attack, Tonkin requested immediate RAF support. The task fell to 140 Wing, 464 and 487 Squadrons, with 107 Squadron from 138 Wing in support. For once there was no doubting the results. When six 107 Squadron aircraft arrived 45 minutes after the main attack, they saw smoke billowing up to a height of some 4,000ft. OC B Flight, Squadron Leader Tom McPhee's efforts that evening exemplified the leadership qualities implicit in the award of a DFC just five days later;[179] recognition too, no doubt, of his contribution to Operation Jericho four months earlier.

Babbage's own efforts that night pale rather into insignificance. He was unable to see whether his attack on a rail bridge over a road was successful. But at least he returned safely at 0300 after nearly three hours in the air – more than can be said for two of his colleagues. An hour and ten minutes later, after nearly three hours airborne, Flight Lieutenant S.T. Sharpe and his navigator, Flying Officer A. Mercer were seriously injured when they crash-landed their damaged aircraft at Tangmere. They were rescued and taken immediately to St Richard's Hospital in Chichester. To conclude the story of an eventful night on a brighter note, Wing Commander Iredale had a lucky escape. Attacked by an Me 109 in the early hours of the morning, he returned with no trace of any damage to his aircraft.

After the initial surge of D-Day activity, flying continued at a relatively low rate for a time. Babbage wasn't scheduled the following day, 12 June, when only 11 of the 12 planned sorties were flown. Radio failure on start-up caused the single cancellation. The squadron's main targets were the marshalling yards at Le Mesnil on the Cotentin peninsula, some 20 miles south-south-west of Cherbourg. With the port itself a key US objective, an innovation was introduced that night: American Mitchell bombers dropped flares to support the raid. This greatly assisted the squadron's attacks and ensured their success. The Mosquito VI may have been an excellent gun platform, but night strafing was fraught with danger. Added to the possibility of ricochets and secondary explosions, judgement of height was made more difficult by the erratic behaviour of the altimeter. Once the aircraft's cannons opened up, it became unreliable. Rather than winding down slowly and uniformly as aircraft height reduced, the instrument would freeze for a moment, then suddenly unwind rapidly as it caught up – disconcerting for the navigator as he monitored the attack. It meant that shell-bursts were the most reliable guide to target and hence ground proximity.

Next afternoon saw a visit from a familiar figure, Lord Trenchard. He delivered a talk to all the squadron aircrew prior to that night's operations. Babbage and McIntyre were one of 12 crews who continued the same pattern of staggered take-offs and night interdiction. Airborne at 0050 and heading to the area south-west of Caen once again, they bombed and strafed opportunity targets: a railway junction, train movements plus tell-tale lights suggesting troops camped in a wood. After two-and-a-half hours, they returned safely, as did all their colleagues, the last of them landing 20 minutes or so before sunrise, at 0520.

On reflection, the squadron had done well to notch up 114 sorties in the week since the night of 5/6 June. To put this effort into context, it's worth summarising the progress of the D-Day operation thus far. After their success in establishing individual beachheads at Gold, Juno and Sword (and by 12 June linking to the American beachheads at Omaha and Utah), Montgomery's forces had twice failed to seize the key port city of Caen: first, by direct assault on 7/8 June, and then by envelopment – the Villers-Bocage episode of 13 June, a disastrous attempt to exploit a gap in the German defences west of the city. After a day of fighting in and around the small town of Villers-Bocage and a second day defending a position outside it, the 22nd Armoured Brigade was forced to retreat.

The next attempt to take Caen would come towards the end of the month and involve 464 Squadron directly, rather than as part of the supporting cast. Meanwhile, on 27 June the Americans would finally take Cherbourg, at the north of the Cotentin peninsula. However, it would prove an almost Pyrrhic victory. Thanks to the Germans' comprehensive demolition plans, the port would not function at full capacity until late September. By then, with so many other French and Belgian ports in Allied hands, Cherbourg's place in the overall reinforcement and resupply plan would be relatively insignificant. The strength and indeed the quality of German resistance – brave and brilliant at times – to the Allied advance meant there would be much more for 464 Squadron to do.

Meanwhile, things were about to change at Gravesend.

CHAPTER 15

RELOCATION

The squadron saw no activity on either 14 or 16 June, and only four crews flew on the intervening night. Babbage and McIntyre were not amongst those who attacked the railway yards at Mézidon, barely a dozen miles south-east of Caen, leaving several fires and a train ablaze as evidence of their success. By now, though, flying from Gravesend was becoming an increasingly difficult and dangerous proposition. Since 13 June the drone of aircraft overhead en route to France had been replaced by an altogether different sound, that of the first V-1 attacks on London. With the German terror weapon routing uncomfortably close to the airfield, and sometimes directly overhead, it represented a hazard to operations. No. 140 Wing had no option but to relocate. Its new base was to be Thorney Island, near Portsmouth, but only after an overnight operation on 17 June. After temporary relocation to Dunsfold, near Guildford, the squadron was tasked with providing all-night cover over northern France. Babbage and his navigator were one of 16 crews who successfully attacked road and railway targets in the vicinity of Cherbourg. This further support operation for the American troops began at 2300, with Babbage taking off at 0025 for a two-hour 50-minute sortie; the last landing came at 0335.

The squadron's aircraft arrived at their new base around noon next day to find it a hive of activity. The first MT convoy of personnel and equipment had arrived mid-morning (a second would appear in the early evening), and tents were already being erected – a task made difficult by a combination of strong winds and firm ground. In the circumstances it was a relief to all concerned to receive only limited tasking that night. Four crews attacked the usual target sets at widely dispersed locations: from Dreux, 40 miles west of Paris, to Le Mans, 90 miles south-south-west of Caen. With no operations on 19 June, Babbage and McIntyre were one of 16 crews who attacked a similarly diverse set of locations the following night: Chartres, the Alençon–Le Mans road and several villages south-west of Paris, one of them surprisingly close to the outskirts. They were the last crew to land, at 0415, after strafing MT convoys near just such a village. While every crew returned safely, Flight Lieutenant Rollo and his navigator, Flying Officer Haward, were fortunate to do so. They crashed on landing but emerged unscathed after flak damage left them with only one engine and virtually no aileron control.

Babbage took part in a similar 16-aircraft raid the following night, 21 June, where many of the attacks on MT and railways took place within 15 miles of the centre of Paris. While a number of aircraft used flares to illuminate their targets, those closer to Paris, particularly the south-west, ran the risk of illumination by searchlight. Babbage, some 40 miles out in the same direction, targeted a railway junction at Dreux but was unable to confirm the results. At the end of the night's operations, one crew was unaccounted for: Flight Lieutenant John Martin and Sergeant Hayden Morgan were posted missing. It eventually emerged that they'd been killed when their aircraft crashed near the hamlet of Balagny-sur-Aunette, some 25 miles north-east of Paris.

The night of 22 June brought a new, sharper focus to the squadron's raids. Target locations were concentrated some 50 miles to the east of Caen. Despite all efforts to inhibit their progress, 2nd SS Panzer Corps, in the shape of the 9th and 10th SS Divisions, was continuing on its way to relieve the defenders there. For the rest of the month the emphasis would be on constant harassment, inhibiting the movement of these reinforcements. This was certainly Babbage's focus during a two-hour 15-minute sortie where he bombed a railway junction. He was the last of 11 aircraft to take off, at 0200, and the last to land, at 0415. The flak defences that evening were reassuringly typical of recent sorties and varied from 'light' to, in Babbage's case, 'meagre'. No-one was aware of it at the time, but the Allies' harassment tactics were meeting with only limited success. The Panzers heading for Normandy may have been severely delayed – river bridges were down, road and railway junctions had been destroyed – but they'd incurred few losses of materiel. Importantly, they retained their combat power.

There now follows a fallow period for Babbage and his navigator. The sortie they flew on the night of 22 June would be their last for over three weeks. There's no obvious reason for this and it would be unwise to speculate. That said, like all 464 Squadron Mosquito aircrew, Babbage and McIntyre were a constituted crew; they always flew together. The demanding nature of their primary task, night interdiction, put a premium on the trust and familiarity that develops between pilot and navigator. It would thus make little sense to split the pair up should one of them be unavailable for any reason – injury or sickness, for example.

Their absence from the flying programme came at a critical time for Overlord. Barely two weeks after the D-Day landings the operation had reached a critical stage, with ground forces struggling to reach their immediate objectives: Caen for Montgomery and the Cotentin peninsula, where Cherbourg was the prize, for the Americans under Lieutenant General Omar Bradley.[180] With his squadron very much part of the Overlord story, the narrative of progress continues during this brief hiatus for Babbage.

Meanwhile, back at Thorney Island, the arrival on 22 June of Squadron Leader Gordon 'Peter' Panitz RAAF, together with his navigator, Flight Lieutenant 'Dickie' Williams, another Australian, presaged a change of command. With the departure of the popular and respected Wing Commander Iredale, together with his navigator, Flight Lieutenant McCaul, Panitz would take over on 28 June.

Operational tasking was now both intermittent and inconsistent: 12 sorties on 23 June and only two the following night. Then on 25 June came an unusual task: a daylight reconnaissance of the Cherbourg area. Squadron Leader McPhee reported there were poles obstructing the runway of Cherbourg-Maupertus airfield, as it happened, the proposed location for the stillborn Operation Airthief. His mission was a precursor to the end of organised resistance in Cherbourg, although it would be a few more days before the Americans mopped up the final elements of opposition at Cap de la Hague, at the north-west tip of the Cotentin peninsula. For the five aircraft tasked later that night, and the pair the previous evening, the focus was mainly on targets within 20-30 miles of Caen. The same was true of the 16 sorties launched on 27 June. Strong winds and heavy rain meant there was no tasking next day, but on 29 June things were set to change.

The catalyst came three days before, on the morning of 26 June, with the start of Operation Epsom, Montgomery' s latest attempt to take Caen. Again, things did not go well. 464 Squadron's role in all this was as part of a major operation with 487 Squadron on the night of 29 June – too late as it turned out. The two 140 Wing squadrons launched 16 aircraft each in a coordinated attack on targets in the area of Villers-Bocage, the village just west of Caen where Montgomery's previous plans had come to grief. Despite light flak, 464's results were encouraging: vehicles strafed, a series of fires with thick black smoke seen rising, all within a five-mile radius of the town and close to the Panzers' front line. But it was all to no avail. Montgomery called a halt to the operation the very next day, 30 June, by which time VIII Corps had lost over 4,000 men.

The squadron ORB for June 1944 concludes with an interesting footnote. One of returning crews on the night of 29 June saw a number of V-1s approaching Littlehampton, a few miles to the east of the airfield. But for all the Mosquito's speed, and perhaps because it was dark, it was unable to catch the doodlebugs.

Babbage and McIntyre returned to the flying programme on 18 July. What follows is a summary of the key developments at squadron level in the interim – a period that began with unseasonally poor weather which made life under canvas damp and uncomfortable, and resulted in the cancellation of a number of operations. With one or two notable exceptions, night operations in support of the Allied landings followed the same pattern as before.

The first incident of note came on 3 July. During a night take-off Flying Officer W.H. Tonkin swung off the runway and ran into a parked Lancaster. While he and his navigator, Flying Officer L.C. Webb, were unharmed, both aircraft were written off in an expensive accident where, fortunately, no-one else was injured. Another aircraft was lost the following night. Flying Officers E.H. 'Ern' Dunkley and H.P. 'Woody' Woodward took off at midnight but failed to return. In taking up the story of another lucky escape, Dunkley also provides an insight into the sort of operation that was now Babbage's stock in trade:

> "We patrolled a railway line at a couple of thousand feet on a good moonlit night, and came across a train that was just begging to be attacked. We promptly obliged them but got the worst end of the stick by a long way. The Germans were very good at coming up with answers to RAF methods. Attacks on trains were giving them more than a few problems, so they introduced flak cars between every ten or so trucks in an effort to stop this sort of attack.[181] On this occasion we were shot up very badly before we got very far with the train and lost one engine. It was running away at take-off revs, about 3,000 rpm, and for some inexplicable reason, every time I tried to turn the petrol off the engine would catch fire. I doused it on two occasions but then decided not to risk running out of fire extinguisher in case it really caught on fire. We set course for home with it still thundering around at 3,000 rpm.
>
> "On our course home there were some 4,000ft mountains and a 100 miles of Channel to Thorney Island. The Allies held an area about 30 miles along the coast and about ten miles deep bounded on the eastern side by the Orne River and Cherbourg on the other. There was one aerodrome in this area which was designated a 'prang aerodrome' for anyone who could not get home. We called them up and couldn't get an answer out of them, and we didn't like the idea of ditching halfway across the Channel, so we decided to bail out. To get out of the Mosquito you jettison the access door, sit on the edge of the hole and then dive out. There was a kick-strip which stood up about an eighth of an inch and every time my navigator (Flying Officer Woodward) tried to wriggle out, the parachute would get caught on this strip. I finally planted my foot in his back and got him out, but that was only half the bother as I then had to get myself out. Every time I took my hand off the control column the aeroplane tended to roll, so I cut both engines, trimmed it slightly nose down and went out the door in a dive.

"A westerly wind took my navigator towards the enemy lines but fortunately he landed in our forward lines. I landed about 3 a.m. amongst a lot of Polish and French-Canadian soldiers who thought I was the forerunner of a parachute invasion or counter attack. I couldn't do very much as I had fractured a leg. They all thought I was a 'Hun' but eventually an English fellow came along and got me out of trouble and I was sent to a forward casualty clearing station. Next morning in the next cot there was a bloke who was injured 'by some . . . who pranged a Mosquito or something about 50 yards from where I was billeted and nearly killed me. If I ever catch up with the bloke that bailed out and just left the aircraft going . . .!'"[182]

While Dunkley remained out of action for a couple of months with a fractured ankle, his navigator was back with the squadron the following day, none the worse for his experience. The same was true, remarkably, of another crew who crash-landed at base that night after suffering flak damage. Flying Officer D.V. Avery and Warrant Officer J.J. Williams emerged unharmed from another write-off. They were back flying again three days later. In the crew context, despite his almost immediate return from Normandy, Ern Dunkley's navigator, Woody Woodward, didn't fly again for over a month.

Other matters of note during Babbage's absence from the operational flying programme included promotion for the new boss; as of 6 July he became Wing Commander G. Panitz DFC. Then on 7 July Flying Officers R.G. Rowell and C.E. Davidson were hit by flak and lost an engine over France. They made it back to Ford airfield, familiar to Babbage from his time at Westhampnett, where they survived a crash landing unharmed; in fact, they were back in the air again two nights later. There was an unusual daylight sortie the following day: a late afternoon reconnaissance of the Normandy landing areas by Flight Lieutenant W.D. Parsons. He was tasked with giving a war reporter named Murray-Edwards a view of the battle area. It's a reflection of the lack of airborne opposition – the Allies' air supremacy – that such a sortie could be flown at all, let alone in daylight.

But the most notable event by far during Babbage's absence from the flying programme was a raid on a Gestapo barracks deep inside France – a raid which once again he was disappointed to have missed.

CHAPTER 16

REVANCHE VENUE DU CIEL, THE REVENGE RAID

In more than the obvious sense, 14 July 1944 would prove an auspicious day – and a busy one for OC 464 Squadron in particular. Together with two other squadron members,[183] Wing Commander Panitz was at RAF Hartford Bridge, north of Newcastle, for a Field Investiture. After he and his navigator, Flight Lieutenant Williams, received their DFCs from HM King George VI, they flew back to Thorney Island to take part in a dusk raid against a Gestapo barracks at Bonneuil-Matours, north-east of Poitiers. In echoes of the Amiens prison raid, four aircraft from 464, together with others from 487 and 21 Squadrons, took part in a precision, low-level attack. In another Amiens parallel, Flight Lieutenant Ted Sismore was part of the planning team; but this time he flew on the mission, with Wing Commander 'Reg' Reynolds.[184] It was led by Pickard's replacement as OC 140 Wing, Group Captain Peter Wykeham-Barnes.[185]

Panitz's formation took off at 2055, an hour-and-a-quarter before sunset, for a sortie of nearly four hours, penetrating some 200 miles into France. The attack left the barracks 'enveloped in flames'. The fascinating story behind this brilliantly successful raid on the Château de Méréville is summarised by a small plaque nearby. It's on the wall of a school next to a bridge over the River Vienne and translates thus:

> 14 July 1944
> Operation "Revenge from the Air"
> Destruction of the SS camp of Bonneuil-Matours by the English aircraft without civilian victims in reprisal for the massacre of English SAS and Resistance fighters.

The raid was requested on 5 July by Captain John Tonkin, leader of the SAS team that some five weeks earlier pinpointed the fuel train near Châtellerault, subsequently destroyed by Babbage's colleagues. Tonkin had been operating with just a handful of colleagues since disaster befell Operation Bulbasket two days before. Throughout their time behind the lines his sizeable team changed locations regularly. Ten days earlier, on 25 June, when the well that was their only water supply failed, they'd been forced to return to a previous camp in a forest near Verrières, south-east of Poitiers. At the time it comprised some 40 SAS troopers, an American Mustang pilot, Second Lieutenant Lincoln Bundy, who'd been shot down on 10 June, and ten Maquisards. But their location had been compromised and in the early morning of 3 July they were encircled and attacked by German troops.

Tonkin was one of the few who escaped, together with three Frenchmen. One wounded officer, Lieutenant Tomos Stephens, was bludgeoned to death by a German officer with the butt of a gun. (It was Stephens who carried out the reconnaissance for the Châtellerault train attack – a round trip of more than 70 miles by bicycle.) The seven Maquisards captured were shot on the spot. Those taken prisoner, including the American pilot, were initially imprisoned. Then, after being forced to dig their own graves, on 7 July all 31 were executed. Meanwhile, the three SAS men who'd been hospitalised were killed by lethal injection.[186] These atrocities were the further consequences of

Hitler's Commando Order. While in no way excusing such actions, they put into perspective the orders given to SAS teams parachuted into France. They were to take no prisoners, albeit the reasoning behind this stricture was less obviously malevolent.

As for the resourceful Tonkin, he not only managed to destroy any secret material, but together with those others of his team who escaped, the 24-year-old continued his disrupting activities for a further month before flying back to the UK. With him were the last five members of his squadron – plus he confided to a friend and erstwhile colleague, Kevin Walton,[187] the individual he suspected had betrayed them, who was being returned for court-martial. For a man who'd previously earned an MC in Italy, a Mention in Dispatches for Tonkin's work behind the lines in France seems scant reward. Walton, who as a holder of both the GC and DSC knew a thing or two about courage, wrote of the marine:

> "That he had been privileged to have crossed paths with some remarkable natural leaders in all walks of life, from full admirals to tramps. There is no doubt that Tonkin heads the lot. He was a remarkable leader and a remarkable man."[188]

The raid was planned for Bastille Day to boost French morale. 2TAF assigned the task to No. 2 Group, where the AOC, Basil Embry, took a particularly close interest and spoke to all the crews involved beforehand. He was keen for it not to be seen as immediate retribution, lest it should lead to further French suffering. Tonkin had identified the barracks where those responsible for the atrocity were housed and the resulting attack was planned with great care. On the outbound leg in daylight the Mosquitos would be escorted by a dozen Mustangs. And by attacking at dusk they would catch the barracks full at the time of the evening meal; they could then escape afterwards in darkness. Importantly, the plan was to attack from the east to avoid civilian casualties in the nearby village.

Munitions were chosen to ensure maximum carnage. The first four Mosquitos were armed with HE bombs, the next wave dropped incendiaries (the RAF's first use of napalm), while the third followed up with another wave of HE bombs – after which the aircraft returned to strafe the blazing target area. With reports of between 80 and 200 Germans killed, and no subsequent reprisals in the area, the raid was an unqualified success. Meanwhile the atrocity itself is commemorated to this day by a road sign in Verrières, *Rue du 3 Juillet 1944*.

With no operations for the next three days, Babbage and McIntyre returned to the fray on 18 July, taking off at 2330 for a sortie of nearly three hours. Targets were the usual 'bridges, roads and railways', but as so often, all 17 aircraft found that it was impossible to confirm the results of their bombing and strafe attacks 'owing to bad visibility'. It was very much the same story the following night. They were one of 16 crews who took part in a similar operation, attacking targets near the eastern outskirts of Caen. Once more there were frustratingly few positive results to report. That said, every aircraft returned safely after sorties approaching three hours again. On 23 July it was the same 'no results seen' story as Babbage bombed a road/rail crossing as part of a 13-aircraft raid. Despite limited confirmation of their success, these Mosquito attacks were having an effect. The main difficulties the Germans faced in responding to the Normandy invasion remained 'the systematic preparations . . . the smashing of the main lines of communication, particularly the railway junctions'.[189]

Babbage would not fly for the next two days. There were no tasks on the first of these but on the second, 25 July, 12 aircraft set off for France at the usual staggered intervals. Only 11 returned. Flying Officers J.R.C. Walton and C.H. Harper were missing. Both survived the loss of their aircraft, but it was some time before their story emerged. They owed their lives and eventual recovery to the Maquis. They lived with a band of guerillas from the French Resistance for a time before returning to England a month or so later.

There was palpable excitement about some of the targets for the squadron's missions the following night. They would be deep inland, attacking trains believed to be carrying V-1 flying bombs. At 2230 Babbage's was the first of 11 aircraft to take off, the vast majority of whom would fly sorties of three hours or more. For once there was visible evidence of success – spectacular at times – albeit not in Babbage's case. It was the usual 'no results seen' after he bombed what he assumed to be a troop encampment in a wood, given away by flickering lights. Like most attacks, his efforts paled into insignificance by comparison with those of Flying Officers W.R. Hurst and W.R. Binks. Theirs, on a crossing, produced fires and a huge explosion, the force of which was felt up to 5,000ft. Positive results were seen too by Flying Officers Rowell and Davidson, who strafed vehicles and then bombed a 20-wagon train.

The following night Babbage and McIntyre were amongst 14 crews who provided target cover deep into France for the latter part of the night. First take-off was at 0125 and last at 0340. Babbage took off at 0300 and landed at 0550, just before dawn. Five of his colleagues had the luxury of landing in daylight. If results were as usual hard to discern, the next evening, 28 July, represented a change of fortune. Covering the early part of the night for once, almost all the squadron's 15 aircraft saw positive results, not least Babbage. He and McIntyre bombed a stationary train and followed up their hits by strafing it too. But they missed the last major effort of the month the following night. It was an important one too.

The American breakout effort across the Cotentin peninsula towards Avranches, the gateway to Brittany and the Atlantic ports to the west, was in full swing and German defences were seen to be weakening. On the night of 29 July the squadron flew 14 sorties, targeting the area around Avranches and Granville where explosions, fires and burning trucks were observed. This compounded the pressure on German troops already suffering in the face of daylight raids from RAF Typhoons and American P-47 Thunderbolts.

In the wake of the eventual American breakout beyond Avranches, the squadron's target sets remained the same, but the pace of operations varied. This was in part due to unseasonally poor weather. There was particular disappointment for the squadron on 1 August. A daylight raid on a barracks at Poitiers housing SS troops went the way of the other two 140 Wing squadrons. In fact, it was a double disappointment because a follow-up raid on the same target that night was also cancelled, albeit for the best of reasons: the success of another rapidly planned and brilliantly executed attack, instigated once again by Captain Tonkin and his SAS survivors.

The next night Babbage and McIntyre bombed a Normandy road junction as part of a 14-sortie raid on targets in the German rear. Taking off at 0050 they were airborne for two hours 45 minutes, typical for sorties to the area around Caen. Little did they realise, they were about to begin their most intensive period of operations – coincident with the start of the Allies' advance across north-west Europe.

Only six sorties were flown on 3 August, but Babbage was airborne again the following night on another 14-aircraft raid. He bombed a ten-carriage troop train, scoring direct hits, then followed up with cannon and machine-gun attacks. Although the ORB records 'A splendid night's work, one of the best we have had recently', it was marred by another loss. At the end of the night one crew was unaccounted for, the Australians Flying Officer A.E. Crellin and Flight Sergeant T.A. Orr. They'd joined the squadron just a few days earlier, on 26 July, and were on only their fourth operation. The other point of note that night is the reappearance in the ORB of a familiar name, Wing Commander Iredale, who 'paid us a visit and combined business with pleasure, joining our raiding party'. He flew a three-hour sortie, taking off at 0035.

Now a staff officer at HQ 2 Group, Mongewell Park, Iredale's responsibilities included all 2TAF's night operations. A pastoral visit to his old unit would therefore have been in order. But given that he'd been away from operations for over a month and was no longer part of a constituted crew – a critically important factor in the demanding low-level night-attack role – this seems questionable practice, even for a man with his experience. Moreover, the navigator he flew with that night, Squadron Leader Robertson, was another 'guest', an unfamiliar name to boot. Setting aside that such a sortie effectively deprived others of valuable experience, more significantly, it placed Peter Panitz in a difficult position. How did the current boss feel about his popular predecessor returning to fly with his erstwhile colleagues? We will never know. Babbage had seen this sort of thing before, of course – when Colin Gray made a successful 'guest appearance' with 41 Squadron at Merston three years earlier. While in Gray's case there were no crew or even hierarchical implications, there was the related issue of adapting to operating with an unfamiliar squadron.

What these two separate examples highlight is a relatively casual attitude to supervision, certainly by modern standards. But priorities were different in wartime. There's another factor too. Both these individuals, Iredale an

Australian and Gray a New Zealander, had come from the other side of the world to fight another nation's battle. This alone warrants respect and may explain why such events appear to have been viewed through a Nelsonian eye.

With no squadron operations on 5 August, Babbage's next sortie, one of 13 the following night, was relatively short, at one hour and 40 minutes. It reflected attacks by the majority of crews on an area from the north-west to the south of Caen, including a number of Seine crossings. However, at least one crew bombed targets much further inland, in the area near Poitiers where what remained of Tonkin's SAS team continued to operate until that very night. Babbage didn't fly the following night, 7 August, which was marked by the loss of another crew, killed in action near the Orne bridgehead, south-west of Caen: Flight Sergeants G.M. Miller RAAF and A. Lister. It was the all-too-familiar demise of a relatively inexperienced crew, albeit 'they were settling down splendidly to the job in hand'. Their first operational sortie had been on 20 July, and this was only their seventh.

Next night, 8 August, Babbage was one of 14 crews who attacked targets in the same area near Caen. In addition to the usual objectives – railways, marshalling yards and Seine crossings – Babbage bombed a flak battery. Twenty-four hours later he was part of a 12-aircraft raid where cloud prevented crews from seeing any results; they were bombing troops thought to be located in woods close to the German lines.

After a standdown on 10 August, next night Babbage was part of an 11-aircraft raid that followed the same familiar pattern: take-off at 0050 to attack targets in the German rearguard, in his case a road/rail junction. He and Flight Sergeant Williams were the last pilots to take off but by the time they returned bad weather prevented a recovery to Thorney Island. Both diverted to Finmere, near Buckingham, and returned the next day. Little did they realise that a long and taxing night lay ahead. Separately that evening, Squadron Leader K.D. Taute and Sub Lieutenant H.H. Becker carried out a special task with the Mosquitos of 151 Squadron: an attack on a tank repair depot south of Paris. Most of their delay-fused bombs fell beyond the target – hardly surprising given that they bombed from 20ft! What was surprising was their routing: coasting in at Gravelines, near Calais, where there was always heavy flak. Since crews would have been aware of this, it seems unnecessarily risky.

On 12 August the squadron began 'turn round' operations, where several crews flew two sorties on the same night, putting a strain on resources, both human and materiel. It effectively amounted to 'overtime', a situation exacerbated by a number of crews approaching their tour-expiry point. (This may explain the temporary reappearance on the flying schedule of Woody Woodward, who on 6 August replaced Flying Officer Davidson as Flying Officer Rowell's navigator; 11 days later they both disappear from view.) The imminent arrival of three new crews would help ameliorate this difficult situation – one that arose in response to a partial German retreat. The Allies were finally making progress, which led to heavy targeting beyond the beachhead. That night the squadron flew 28 sorties.

Babbage and McIntyre were one of 12 crews who flew twice. Their first take-off came at 0015. With only 35 minutes between landing and their second sortie at 0415, when they finally landed at 0610 they were exhausted. Their reward – as for almost all their colleagues' own bombing and strafe attacks that night – was tangible proof of success for once: smoke, fire, sparks and explosions.

It was the same thing 24 hours later, although this time they were able to take a breather between sorties. First take-off was 0120 but they had an hour and 35 minutes before the next, at 0415. This time, though, there was little reward for effort because of poor visibility in the target area. But there was the satisfaction of seeing the squadron notch up 34 sorties, with 16 crews flying twice. With aircrew under increased operational pressures and ground crew working long shifts, it was a considerable relief when operations returned to a single night wave next day. That said, what followed was another hiatus for Babbage and McIntyre. There's no obvious reason why, but it was ten days – eventful ones at that – before they returned to operations.

The next three days saw the squadron conduct single waves of night operations that followed broadly the same pattern as before. However, 17 and 18 August brought a return to two-night waves: 34 sorties on 17 August, with 14 crews flying twice, and 24 the following day, which meant only five crews doubled up. With no operations on either 19 or 21 August due to bad weather, on the 20th came another special task that Babbage would again dearly love to have flown. With the German presence in Normandy reduced by now to a pocket seven miles wide by six miles deep, the squadron was tasked with a daylight raid on a target in an entirely different area, some 400 miles inland from the French coast: the railway marshalling yards at Chagny, near Dijon, where a concentration of ammunition and supply trains had been reported. The 12-aircraft bombing and strafe attack was led by OC 464 and carried out at extreme low level – 'zero ft'. In terms of the damage that resulted, the raid was an unqualified success. But sadly, it cost the lives of Wing Commander Panitz and Flight Lieutenant Williams. While no one saw their demise, several aircraft were hit by intense and accurate flak from nearby Le Creusot. This was assumed to be the cause.

In wartime things move quickly. When Babbage returned to operations next day the squadron already had a new boss, Wing Commander 'Bill' Langton.[190] Having been attached to the squadron since July, and with an Australian pedigree, he proved a popular choice to replace a man who had more than proved himself during his two short months in command, as indeed had his navigator, Dickie Williams. They'd flown together since their time on 456 Squadron (another RAAF unit), where Panitz earned his reputation as a 'train-buster'.

For the remainder of August the squadron continued with single night waves of staggered individual sorties, albeit focussed on new target areas to the north and east of the Somme. It was a busy period for Babbage and McIntyre; they flew six sorties in nine days. On 23 August, during a relatively shallow penetration into France, a sortie of only one hour and 50 minutes, they located targets on a road. Fires and explosions suggested their bombing and strafe attacks found their mark. Others did similarly well in the Seine area, bombing and strafing vehicles and even the occasional barge. They were one of 15 crews involved that night, as they were 24 hours later when they targeted the same area, close to Rouen, in a longer mission of two-and-a-quarter hours. After bombing a road, Babbage strafed a number of vehicles, with the satisfying sight of flames erupting as his rounds struck home.

During a short one-hour 25-minute sortie to the Caen area the following night, 25 August, Babbage and 12 other crews again saw encouraging results from their attacks: vehicles blown up, fires started plus multiple flashes and explosions. It suggested that the squadron was continuing to make life difficult for the retreating German ground forces. The following night brought a variation in the squadron's targeting. Babbage was part of a 17-aircraft wave. While he bombed roads, others took on railways, multi-car trains and even an airport 50 miles north of Paris, Beauvais-Tille. Then on 27 August, he and McIntyre were one of the only two crews to be tasked – relatively late on at that. They took off at 0450. The other aircraft, flown by Flying Officer C.H.L. Foster, was airborne five minutes later but developed unserviceabilities and returned early without carrying out any attacks. Babbage targeted marshalling yards but, frustratingly, he was again unable to see the results of his efforts; he landed at sunrise, 0700. Unlike Foster, who got to bed a lot earlier, he failed to appear on the following day's programme – raids by 15 aircraft on Seine crossings and as far east as the Strasbourg marshalling yards. With no operations on 29 August, he also missed a 14-aircraft raid next day targeting areas north of the Somme.

To conclude a month that would go down in Babbage's logbook as his busiest yet on operations – nearly 36 hours in the air – he and McIntyre were amongst the 15 crews who contributed to a significant event on 31 August: the squadron's first penetration into Germany. All the targets were in the Saarbrucken area, where Babbage bombed a railway. While he returned unscathed, as did all his colleagues, there was damage to his aircraft. It occurred, unbeknown to him, when he jettisoned the drop tanks he was carrying – a necessary precaution given that it was a round trip of some 800 miles. He landed at 0420 after a three-hour 40-minute sortie – his longest thus far. That said, two others that night racked up four hours in the cockpit. It's hard to imagine the tension crews must have felt during such a lengthy period at relatively low level at night over hostile territory. They doubtless slept well afterwards – the net effect of exhaustion and relief.

At the end of an intensive month's flying, there was good news to accompany the release of some remarkable statistics. This came on 29 August when the squadron learned that Flying Officer Bob Walton, shot down on 26 July, was back in London. (That said, he would subsequently be repatriated to Australia, deemed 'medically unfit'.) While there was no news yet of his navigator, Flying Officer Charles Harper, it would later emerge that he'd arrived back in the UK on 23 August.

The statistics were produced to mark two years since 464's formation (records began on 27 August 1942); the ORB for August 1944 summarised the squadron's achievements thus far. With an early reference to Wing Commander Iredale's visit that combined business with pleasure happily signed off by the new boss – it was outside his bailiwick, of course – it notes that the squadron had flown 3,969 hours and 909,706 miles on operations.[191] In 1,776 sorties crews had damaged two enemy ships and 11 enemy aircraft; however: 'It's impossible to give an accurate number of the numbers of M/T, trains etc. that have been damaged or destroyed.' Touché!

The bad weather that plagued Operation Overlord almost throughout was back with a vengeance at Thorney Island in September. Heavy rain and gale-force winds up to 60 mph at the beginning of the month forced the squadron to abandon its tented facilities and set up in a hangar, while taking up accommodation in various messes. The appalling conditions led to the cancellation of operations on three successive nights, 2-4 September. With a stand-down to follow, there was then frustration over the lack of tasking on 6 and 7 September. Partial compensation came on the 7th with the unheralded arrival of Flight Lieutenant Donald Shanks, who'd gone missing after bailing out of Squadron Leader Oxlade's aircraft on 5 June. He'd been back in the country for a week or so and his reappearance at the squadron, albeit briefly, was a real fillip for his colleagues. They were less happy, however, with confirmation that his pilot had almost certainly been killed in the crash from which Shanks narrowly escaped.

Babbage's is the first name to appear in the 464 ORB for September – but not until the 8th. Even then the weather was 'foul over the Channel' as eight aircraft set off that night to bomb the ferry crossings at Walcheren, on the Scheldt estuary in Belgium. His sortie with McIntyre was logged as a 'near miss'. He aimed to attack a road/rail bridge but watched his bombs fall into a canal 25 yards north of the target. When he and McIntyre landed back at Thorney Island at 0250 after a sortie of two hours and 45 minutes, it was the last time they would fly in a Mosquito together.

At this point McIntyre disappears from 464 Squadron's records entirely, while Babbage flies twice more: an NFT the next day and a ferry to Staverton,

Gloucester, the day after. While there's no mention of the crew's departure, or the reasons for it, there's nothing unusual in this. Indeed, it's consistent with the way many of 464 Squadron's arrivals and departures are dealt with in the ORB – bar those of executives and any resulting from unusual circumstances. That said, for Babbage's final sortie to go unremarked on what according to the ORB was a 'Quiet day of beautiful weather. Very little doing at all,' seems less than he deserved.

Before dealing briefly with his subsequent career, it's worth summarising his time as a Mosquito pilot. Between 9 May and 8 September 1944 Babbage flew 33 sorties and 99 hours 40 minutes on operations, almost exclusively at night – over half the hours he accumulated on type. But figures tell only part of the story. He would have flown few more stressful sorties than those that summer. The night, low-level intruder role was one of the most demanding in the RAF's wartime inventory. Babbage and McIntyre were fortunate to survive their experiences on 464 Squadron; so many of their Australian colleagues did not.

CHAPTER 17

THE POST-WAR YEARS

According to Babbage's record of service, he was posted to No. 140 Wing on 5 September 1944 – five days before his final sortie with 464 Squadron. To compound this apparent inconsistency, his Form 1406 indicates that the very next day he was posted supernumerary to 83 Group Communications Squadron, part of 2TAF at Eindhoven, in the Netherlands. The explanation probably lies in an increasingly relaxed approach to both administration and supervision as the war draws to a close. It was a time of uncertainty too. Those like Babbage, released from the front line, often found their careers in limbo.

He certainly felt that way when his next tour began in relatively mundane fashion, flying communications aircraft (the Anson and Auster); however, for a man who simply loved flying, it would soon offer more exciting opportunities. They came with his change of status: from supernumerary to a flying appointment in the acting rank of squadron leader. On 15 February 1945 he was appointed OC 83 Group Communications Squadron. In the months that followed, the sheer variety of aircraft Babbage flew makes impressive reading. In addition to the Anson and Auster, he logged time in the Messenger, Proctor, Typhoon and various marks of Spitfire as well as a number of captured German aircraft: the Fieseler (Fi) 156 Storch, Fi 256, Ju 52 and Siebel Si 204.

In amongst all this excitement, the 28-year-old finally found time to repay the loyalty of his fiancée. On 28 June 1945, at the parish church of St Mary's, Bathwick, Squadron Leader Cyril Babbage DFM, AE, RAFVR married Mary Joan Brown. What the new Mrs Babbage, three years his junior, felt about the moves, absences and uncertainties that followed hardly bears thinking about.

First came what would on paper have been Babbage's dream appointment. On 9 August 1945 he was posted as OC 245 Squadron, a 2TAF Typhoon unit at Schleswig, in Germany. But there was a catch. The very next day the squadron was disbanded. His task was simply to manage the unit's administrative run-down. On the day of its disbandment, the squadron was re-formed as a Meteor unit back in the UK. At RAF Colerne, 504 Squadron was re-numbered as 245 to form part of the RAF's first wing of jet fighters. A month later, his job done, Babbage was posted to HQ 83 Group, also at Schleswig.

With the RAF transitioning to the jet age, and plans to reduce the service considerably in size with the end of the war, personnel staffs had little option but to put Babbage into a holding pattern of temporary appointments, albeit posts where he still managed to fly regularly. If he had concerns about the future, he was not alone. Many were in a similar position. Some were even worse placed, not least those from overseas like the Australians with whom he flew. No. 464 Squadron was disbanded on 25 September 1945, the day after its Mosquitos were flown to Woodhall Spa to be placed in storage.

Seven months after his posting to HQ 83 Group, on 11 April 1946 Babbage was moved to another staff appointment, at HQ No. 2 Group, RAF Gütersloh. But by the end of the year he was heading back to the training world. On 1 November he joined No. 21 (Pilot) Advanced Flying Unit, first at Wheaton Down and then Moreton-in-Marsh, in preparation for his return to instructing at No. 22 SFTS, Ouston, on 3 February 1947. Less than a year later, on 14 January 1948 he was on the move again, appointed commander of a training squadron and chief flying instructor at No. 22 FTS, Syerston. One incident towards the end of a 20-month tour flying the Harvard and Prentice illustrates vividly the qualities of a man consistently rated above average as an instructor. It led the station commander, Group Captain H.M. David, to hand-write an official letter of commendation.[192] Dated 25 April 1949, it was headed 'Instances of Avoidance by Exceptional Flying Skill or Judgement, of Loss of, or Damage to, Aircraft or Personnel'. As a tribute to a pilot of immense ability, it's worth reproducing in full:

> "Squadron Leader C.F. Babbage was giving an instructor a [Harvard] night recategorisation test.
>
> "On the fourth take-off at a height of 200 feet and an airspeed of 100 knots, the engine gave a loud bang and began to vibrate excessively, flames issued from the top starboard cowling and there was a serious loss of power. Squadron Leader Babbage, who was in the front cockpit, took over control, informed the [control] tower that he was making a crash landing, and realising that the River Trent lay ahead, turned left into the circuit in the hope of landing the aircraft on the airfield. By this time a considerable amount of oil had been thrown on the windscreen and the engine seemed likely to fail completely, so rather than risk a crash landing among the station buildings, he turned left again and carried out a successful crosswind landing on the airfield. He kept the tower informed of his intentions throughout. Owing to the peculiar situation of the airfield, the normal procedure of going straight ahead after engine failure on take-off, is acceptable only as a last resort, since it probably involves crashing into the River Trent.
>
> "Squadron leader Babbage displayed coolness, considerable skill, and sound airmanship in very difficult circumstances."

At the end of a tour during which he was granted a permanent commission guaranteeing service until age 47, on 23 September 1949 Babbage was posted overseas – to Greece as a liaison officer, part of an RAF delegation advising on training. After four months in Athens, he found himself posted to RAF Nicosia, Cyprus, for two years. Then it was back to his first love – flying, and the exciting prospect of commanding a Flying Training Command Meteor squadron. He was back to instructing.

In May 1952 Babbage returned to CFS for two courses at Little Rissington: a brief, three-week 'refresher' on the Harvard and then No. 142 Jet Conversion Course. The latter saw him retain his A2 instructor qualification, this time on the Meteor. All this was to prepare him to take over No. 2 Squadron at 208 Advanced Flying School,[193] RAF Merryfield, near Ilminster in Somerset. The unit's task was to train pilots on Vampires as well as Meteors. There were plenty of dual-control Meteor T.7s when Babbage arrived on 7 August 1952, but it wasn't until early the following year that the first two-seat Vampire T.11 trainers were delivered. Soon he was instructing on both types. Before the T.11s appeared, those converting to the Vampire effectively followed in the footsteps of their early Spitfire predecessors. Their first Vampire sortie was their first solo and it could prove a similarly scary experience. Ralph Swift, 18 at the time, recalled joining 15 Course at Merryfield just a month after Babbage arrived:

> "The Vampire T.11 was not yet in service so we flew dual on the Meteor 7 and were then sat in a Vampire 1 or 3 and launched into the sky. Your first solo was your first flight in a Vampire and it could be tricky when you lowered the flaps, the nose would pitch up sharply. It was a rudimentary aircraft and the instrumentation was definitely piston era. We lost about one pilot per month in training. My pal Johnny Gillard speared in at Curry Rivel[194] one stormy day and is buried at the local churchyard."

Despite the fact that he was no longer flying on operations, the losses that had been a constant feature of Babbage's flying career continued at Merryfield. Successful though the Meteor would prove, it had its vices. Of nearly 4,000 in RAF service, 890 were lost (145 of them in 1953 alone, the first full year of Babbage's appointment), costing the lives of 450 pilots. Amongst the contributory factors were poor brakes, undercarriage failures, short endurance and single-engined handling. Lack of ejection seats in early marks of the aircraft, plus the difficulties of bailing out at high speed, simply exacerbated an already challenging situation.

Babbage remained at Merryfield a little over two years, until his posting on 26 November 1954 to an unidentified Air Ministry unit. It's the first in a series of administrative appointments where there's an element of mystery, not least because it's a Special Duties List (SDL) role, one which brings an additional element of sensitivity and responsibility. Less than five months later he joined the UK contingent supporting an unidentified American operation at Edzel, home to the RAF's 63 Maintenance Unit (MU), an aircraft storage and repair and salvage unit.

Promoted to wing commander on 1 July 1955, two months later to the day he was appointed to command the RAF element at Royal Naval Air Station Evanton, near Invergordon. However, it's listed in his logbook record of service as another Air Ministry SDL role. In 1948 the station had closed as an aircraft storage unit, but it remained in use as a relief landing ground and was eventually leased to the USAF as a 'meteorological balloon site'. While the balloons launched there were ostensibly for meteorological forecasting purposes, many were equipped with cameras – part of the Cold War intelligence-gathering activities. Some of these 'spy balloons' reportedly photographed the Soviet Union. Why either Edzel or Evanton would require an RAF liaison officer or advisor is by no means clear.

A little over two years in an administrative post at RAF Stradishall, from 3 May 1956 to 6 June 1958, follows these appointments then leads to more mystery. First, there's a gap of some four months with no appointment recorded in either his logbook or Form 1406. Next, at the end of October, comes a two-day Senior Officers' Course at the Joint Services Amphibious Warfare Centre. There's then another eight-month gap with no recorded appointments until on 1 July 1958 Babbage is posted to 'D' Unit, RAF West Drayton, as 'Officer Commanding and Liaison Officer'. While the liaison element relates to the USAF (the base hosted the 3911th Air Base Group, part of the USAF's Strategic Air Command), the function of D Unit itself is less clear. All we know is that it was sufficiently important to be one of only three elements retained under RAF control (the others were married quarters and air traffic control accommodation) when West Drayton was transferred to the USAF in 1952. The following year D Unit and the 'RAF Liaison Party' combined to become RAF West Drayton, itself retitled simply as 'D Unit' in 1956. With the demise of RAF Home Command in January 1959, the unit transferred to Technical Training Command. Meanwhile, the redesignated 3911th Combat Support Group remains at West Drayton to this day. None of this is any help in unravelling Babbage's role at West Drayton, of course. The only clue is an old photograph of a dapper wing commander, complete with swagger stick and flanked by RAF policemen, suggesting a representative position of some authority. It's one that leads to a more conventional final appointment.

Babbage's RAF career concludes with a posting as Officer Commanding Administration Wing, RAF Colerne, on 27 November 1961. The base was home to 49 MU at the time, but with the arrival of Hastings aircraft on 1 March 1963, it became a Transport Command airfield. Unremarkable appointment though it was, it provided Babbage with his last few hours in the cockpit of an RAF aircraft and led to an unexpected degree of publicity. In the summer of 1962 he found himself commanding a detachment of some 260 personnel at RAF Larissa in Greece. Its purpose was to provide administration and support for a Parachute Regiment exercise, the precursor to a major and mildly controversial NATO exercise. What made Fallex 62 contentious was a scenario that assumed the third world war would start with a pre-emptive strike on Europe, albeit only partially successful. The real-life situation that Babbage faced was more mundane. A number of poverty-stricken British tourists arrived begging the RAF to fly them home. With others suffering from similar shortages of funds, and with a trickle in danger of becoming a flood, he was unable to help. In fact, earlier 'rescue' missions using Britannia aircraft had been halted in similar circumstances. It was a non-story in some ways, but enough to provide a three-column spread in a Bath newspaper under the headline 'Fly Us Back Ask British Tourists', with a few pictures (including one of Wing Commander Babbage in tropical uniform) and local interest interviews.

When Babbage celebrated his birthday on 27 June 1964 he did so with mixed feelings. He'd reached the point at which the RAF decided on his future. There were two possibilities: extended service to age 55 or release at age 47. Like so many of those who served their country (and in some cases their adopted country) so well in time of war, because he was not expected to reach higher rank, his services were no longer required. If this seems heartless, ungrateful even – and many a decorated veteran felt this way – there was logic behind the policy. It allowed for a regular influx of new blood and ensured there was room for the best and brightest of these to progress to higher rank. Such thoughts, even if they crossed Babbage's mind, would have done nothing to ease the pain of severing links with a service, and a way of life that was all he'd known for more than 25 years.

EPILOGUE

Cyril Babbage was a man of his time, typical in some ways, unusual in others. Typical in that he unhesitatingly answered a nation's call in 1939. Typical too of those who survived their wartime experiences simply because luck was on their side – in his case more than just once. It's hard to overestimate the importance of good fortune to those like Babbage with limited flying hours and little prior Spitfire experience when first thrust into the heat of battle.

Arguably the most unusual thing about him was his first-hand experience of two of the most significant events in the nation's recent history: the Battle of Britain and D-Day. This doesn't necessarily make Babbage unique, but it does make him one of a rare breed. Unusual too was his time with the Australians of 464 Squadron, which highlights the contribution Commonwealth countries made to Britain's war effort. No. 140 Wing included both an Australian and a New Zealand squadron – surrogate homes for men who had travelled from the other side of the world to fight, and all too often die for a common cause. To illustrate this last point, the per capita loss rate for New Zealanders flying with the RAF was double that of Australia and 30 per cent higher than the UK's.

As one of the young Battle of Britain pilots Brian Kingcome described as "typical of their generation", Babbage is unusual because we now know so much more about him – unlike the majority of the nearly 3,000 aircrew

Churchill dubbed 'The Few'. Of these, less than 200 became aces during the Battle of Britain. This alone makes Babbage a rarity. It also puts him in the top five to six per cent of all fighter pilots who served with Commonwealth air forces during the war.[195] If this was unusual, in other ways he was typical of what we know of these brave young men. He drove an open-topped, two-seat MG sports car – one fuelled by the rationed petrol he was allocated simply because he was on operations. And if his meagre petrol allowance proved insufficient, there was always the odd drum of 87-octane available, syphoned from bowsers with the help of squadron ground crew.

Babbage was typical in other ways too. Once the Battle of Britain was over, he delighted in taking the opportunity to overfly the houses of friends and relations, not least the uncle and aunt who moved to the small village of Clun. There he performed victory rolls over the market square with all the exuberance of youth – proof, as if she needed it, that Aunt Gertrude's good luck charm continued to function. This sort of behaviour, albeit behaviour that in some cases bordered fatally on the reckless, is testament to the spirit that sustained young men who faced the prospect of their own mortality every time they climbed into a cockpit. There were echoes of that same spirit when, as a wing commander, Babbage had the singular honour of leading the parade of veterans who marched past Lord Dowding on Horse Guards Parade to celebrate the 20th anniversary of the Battle of Britain.

Another of the themes that run through this personal history is that of loss, of human tragedy. The strength and resilience of the human spirit is nowhere more evident than in the way aircrew dealt with the all-too-regular loss of friends and colleagues. Brian Kingcome recalled the feeling after landing from an early morning scramble: "Behind us a lifetime of emotions, death for some and for those of us safely back on the ground . . . thoughts quickly suppressed of friends not yet accounted for."[196] It was one thing to learn after landing that someone had failed to return. There was always the hope that the individual or crew would eventually turn up, and sometimes they did. But it was another altogether to watch or even hear someone die. There was no training for this. It was something people like Babbage never got used to, no matter how often it happened. And unlike today, there was no support mechanism in the 1940s – just the bond of shared experience.

After a wartime friend, Paul Phillips,[197] was killed indulging his passion for motorcycle racing in 1949, Babbage stayed in touch with his widow Edith for the rest of his life. Concerned to ensure that she and her two children were properly provided for, the thoughtfulness and moral support of 'a nice, quiet man' left a lifelong impression on her.

Babbage's story also brings out the anomalies of life on a fighter squadron, and indeed within the wider RAF as it underwent a major cultural change seen by some as 'revolutionary'.[198] How on earth did pilots cope with what Kingcome described as "the strange, fascinating, schizophrenic world of the fighter pilot"?[199] His solution: "When each night could be our last, we couldn't afford to waste it in sleep. So we partied by night and cat-napped between flights by day."[200] It was this displacement from reality that struck Babbage almost forcibly at times. But it was more than displacement. For some there was almost a sense of guilt. Unlike those who endured the Blitz, aircrew could fight back. Even so, they were conscious of fighting a different war from their army and navy colleagues, whose only experience of home comforts was during rare periods of leave – a situation exacerbated by service overseas, something Babbage experienced only as the war drew to a close.

One of the features that distinguished the RAF from its sister services at the outset was that it was officers who did the fighting. Things changed with the introduction of the RAFVR. It created a unique dynamic: crews comprising airmen, NCOs and officers. To some outside the service this seemed incongruous, yet it worked – most obviously in Bomber Command's larger aircraft, but equally in the Mosquitos that Babbage flew.

To a degree, the effectiveness of a squadron depended on the cohesion of its constituent parts: engineers and aircrew. In the engineering environment, officers acted in a leadership, management or supervisory role; they weren't 'hands-on' practitioners. By contrast, aircrew officers and NCOs worked, and more importantly flew together – a situation that still obtains today. It's to the RAF's credit that such a system functioned effectively from the outset – in a wartime environment too – and continues to do so. Exactly why is difficult to say. Contributory factors doubtless included a clearly defined goal, a common enemy, belief in a cause, mutual respect and, of course, leadership. That these dynamics somehow trumped the obvious impediment of social separation is evident in Babbage's seamless transition from civilian to NCO to junior and, finally, to senior officer.[201]

There's a partial parallel in the existence of elite formations like the SAS, which plays a minor but important role in Babbage's story. Here the success, the survival even, of small teams in particular depended on the same inter-reliance between officers and men found amongst RAF aircrew. One of the most intriguing features of Babbage's tale as it unfolds is the linkage it provides to other events, to other individuals with stories of their own. Some of these he would have been aware of in the general rather than the particular sense, others he would have learned of only after the event, if at all.

We know he was no fan of Douglas Bader, but what impression did Amy Johnson make on him? She certainly captivated his colleagues. And what did he make of Loel Guinness's unexpectedly generous hospitality, or the presence of ladies of society in the YMCA tea-wagon? Did he ever learn what lay behind the identification of those special targets by Tonkin's SAS team? How did it feel to see and hear a doodlebug pass overhead? And finally, how did the taking of another's life affect him? On this last point, as with all the others, we will never know. But it's reasonable to assume that, unlike some with whom he flew, there was no personal animosity towards his German counterparts in the air, or indeed those on the ground he bombed or strafed. If he had any regrets, they would surely have been over the loss of innocent civilian lives – and not just in the Blitz, on the Continent too, the vast majority in France.

If nothing else, Cyril Babbage's inspiring story – the story of an unsung hero, a calm and caring man to whom flying meant so much – illustrates the tragedy, the unintended consequences and the sheer futility of war.

APPENDIX 1

COMBAT REPORTS

To make a claim, pilots involved in an aerial engagement would complete a Form 'F', the Fighter Command Combat Report. It would be collated by the squadron intelligence officer and submitted to HQ Fighter Command for confirmation, or otherwise. The three categories of claim for enemy aircraft were: destroyed, probably destroyed and damaged. On occasions where several pilots shared a claim, proportions, e.g. a half-share, were allocated accordingly. The texts below are exact transcriptions of Babbage's Form 'F' narratives; no attempt has been made to correct syntax, spelling etc. In any event, compilation was the intelligence officer's responsibility; the pilot simply signed off the completed form.

A consolidated list of Babbage's claims can be found in Appendix 2.

SERGEANT C.F. BABBAGE, 602 SQUADRON
18 August 1940

I was Green 3 in 602 Squadron Spitfires which took off from W. Hampnett at 1415 hours. I attacked one Ju87 when making out to sea, part of a general stream. This did skids to escape, but I opened fire silencing rear gunner. I attacked again firing another long burst, E/A dived into sea.

I broke away and as I did so did a No. 2 attack on Me 109 passing overhead. I saw bullets entering its fuselage. I was then at 1000 ft. I landed at W. Hampnett about 1450 hours.

---

25 August 1940

I was Green 2 and took off from W. Hampnett at 1704 hrs. I saw a large number of E/A over Warmwell district. I attacked one Me 110 at same height as myself 10/15 degrees from head on, glass house collapsed and E/A rolled onto back on fire. I broke away and manoeuvred onto tail of Do 17 at 14,000 ft. Fired long burst from slightly above, whereupon starboard engine started smoking and top gun turret disintegrated, & E/A turned back towards land. Attacked again from astern; E/A half rolled & crashed into sea from 12000 feet. I landed at W Hampnett by 1844 hours. One of E/A crew attempted to bail out & I killed him during second burst.

---

26 August 1940

I was Green 2 and took off from W. Hampnett at 1613 hrs. I followed Green 1 climbing to attack fighters and got separated. I saw one Me 109 on tail of Spitfire, and attacked from dead astern and as he turned away used deflection shot. He fell into spin from the turn and went down with copious quantities of black smoke coming from engine. I am confident from the colour and quantity of smoke that this E/A was probably destroyed.

I then attacked centre aircraft of 3 Do 215's[202] in vic formation which was one of several such formations making out to sea, adopting dead astern attack, opening 300 yds and firing until my ammunition was exhausted. I saw my bullets striking this E/A but observed no other damage. Heavy cross fire was experienced from all three bombers, and as I broke away downwards to the left I was struck by a cannon shell probably from a Me 109 and had to bail out because my aircraft was on fire.

---

11 September 1940

I was Blue 2 and followed Blue 1 in attack on Me 110's. One Me 110 before we got within range detached itself from remainder and headed South. I attacked this full beam from 500 feet above on E/A's starboard side, and broke away behind. E/A then turned into sun but I saw it again manoeuvring to attack me. I made head on attack same altitude swinging left to avoid return fire. I climbed into sun, and made another beam attack. E/A dived 45 degrees and I followed till it crashed into sea. I climbed back to 16,000 ft and was attacked by 2 Me 110's which were on a southerly course, one of which I fired at without visible effect (head on); after breaking away I lost sight of E/A and returned to base.

---

15 September 1940

I was Green 2 and took off from W. Hampnett 1433 hrs. One Do 215 was flying 1 mile to starboard of main formation heading South and just above cloud. I made 1 beam attack and observed my bullets striking fuselage. I then made second attack dead astern and pieces dropped off enemy fuselage; perspex hood round rear gunner at rear of pilots compartment was shattered and rear gun ceased fire. I then lost E/A in cloud. During this attack I was hit by machine gun fire and my engine disabled but I was able to land at Shoreham.

---

26 September 1940

I was Green 2 and took off from West Hampnett at 1603 hours. Squadron became separated and I led Green 3 into attack, 30/40 He 111' s but without any result seen. I then went out to sea in a big circle climbing and attacked a Vic of 3 He 111's going South. Selected He 111 on right and attacked quarter ahead. This E/A dropped out of formation and crashed into sea.

---

27 September 1940

I was Green 2 and took off from West Hampnett 0850 hrs. When Squadron was attacked by Me 109's I was myself attacked by 3 Me 109's and went into a steep spiral dive to 500 ft. to avoid them and then saw 1 Ju 88 flying South at 400 ft. at about 200 m.p.h. I attacked this five times full beam and saw this E/A crash into sea.

---

27 September 1940

I was Green 2 and took off from West Hampnett 1510 hrs. When over Dungeness at 15,000 ft on East course, I was attacked from above and behind by 2 Me 109's. I saw them coming and avoided them and one then attacked Blue 3. When it broke away from Blue 3, I attacked it from head on slightly below. I broke away underneath and lost sight of E/A. S/Ldr. Johnstone, leading Squadron as Red 1, saw this E/A going down about 45 degrees dive with heavy black smoke pouring from it and considers it was probably destroyed.

PILOT OFFICER C.F. BABBAGE, 41 SQUADRON
14 August 1941

I took off from Merston aerodrome at 13.50 hrs in the leading section of 41 Squadron. We crossed the English coast at Dungeness and then the French coast N. of Bologne [sic] at 25,000 ft. Orbiting St. Omer several ME 109's were seen above. On crossing the French coast near Gravelines on the way back I noticed two ME 109's tailing No 2 section on our port side so I broke away from the leading section and led Sgt. Glen into the attack. I made one diving attack on one ME 109 from full beam but missed. Only m/gs fired, one cannon fired when bottom button was depressed. I turned to engage enemy aircraft and one more ME 109 joined in and a dogfight ensued. I fired approx. 3 secs burst at one ME 109 on a slight turn and saw my De Wilde hitting enemy aircraft which immediately emitted white glycol smoke and dived away inland at a steep angle. I was unable to follow in the straight dive owing to the 2nd 109 coming in behind me which I turned to engage but it half-rolled and I lost sight of it below me. As I turned for home I noticed the first ME 109 still going down about 5 miles inland emitting a trail of white smoke. Landed at Merston at 15.30 hrs.

---

18 September 1941

I was leading No.3 Section in 41 Squadron and took off from Manston at 0950 hours to cover Blenheims attacking convoy off Ostend. We intercepted several enemy aircraft, one of which fired ineffectively at my No.2 after squadron had broken up. This enemy aircraft appeared to be similar to a Curtiss 75A, but with a slimmer fuselage. The enemy aircraft passed beneath me and I saw crosses on the fuselage. It then turned south at high speed and I followed it at twelve-and-a-quarter pounds boost and 2,800 revs, with the result that I was overhauling slowly, indicated airspeed 350 mph at sea level. I got within range just off Ostend and fired a five-seconds burst with cannon and machine-guns from dead astern. The enemy aircraft broke up and crashed into the sea, confirmed by Pilot Officer Jarred, who followed me.

APPENDIX 2

CLAIMS SUMMARY

DATE	CLAIM	LOCATION	SQUADRON	AIRCRAFT
18 August 1940	Ju 87	Ford airfield	602	Spitfire Mk I
18 August 1940	Me 109 – Damaged	Tangmere	602	Spitfire Mk I
19 August 1940	Ju 88 – quarter share	Tangmere	602	Spitfire Mk I
25 August 1940	Me 110	Dorchester	602	Spitfire Mk I
25 August 1940	Do 17	Dorchester	602	Spitfire Mk I
26 August 1940	Me 109E – Probable	Selsey Bill	602	Spitfire Mk I
11 September 1940	Me 110	5 miles south of Selsey Bill	602	Spitfire Mk I
15 September 1940	Do 215 – Damaged	Beachy Head	602	Spitfire Mk I
26 September 1940	He 111	Southampton Water	602	Spitfire Mk I
27 September 1940	Ju 88	8 miles north of Dungeness	602	Spitfire Mk I
27 September 1940	Me 109E – Probable	Dungeness	602	Spitfire Mk I
12 October 1940	Ju 88 – Probable, third share	Beachy Head	602	Spitfire Mk I
14 August 1941	Me 109F – Damaged	Gravelines	41	Spitfire Mk Vb
18 September 1941	Fw 190[203]	1 mile north of Ostend	41	Spitfire Mk Vb

Totals:

Seven and one shared enemy aircraft destroyed, two and one shared probables and three damaged.

ACKNOWLEDGEMENTS

This book has benefitted greatly from the help provided by a number of individuals. To each and every one of them I owe an enormous debt of gratitude. They're listed below in alphabetical order with two exceptions: first, Francis Wells, without whose help the project would never have seen the light of day. His efforts to learn more about a first cousin once removed were effectively the catalyst for the project; his encouragement and assistance has been invaluable throughout. Moreover, his last-minute tracing of equally helpful family members injected colour into otherwise grey areas – and this thanks to Babbage's daughters, Nina Fergusson and Stella Crocker, son Simon Babbage and grandson Stuart Crocker, the individual through whom the connection was finally made. Second comes the indefatigable Ray Deacon, who spent many an hour working on the illustrations. Almost every photograph required the tender loving care that only an expert could provide, so to him I extend a special word of thanks.

In no way does the foregoing detract from the important contributions of so many others, starting with David Ails, whose splendid painting of Babbage's Fw 190 victory adorns the front cover. If only we knew what lay behind this particular commission. In resolving queries related to Babbage's time on 41 Squadron, Steve Brew was unfailingly helpful. His detailed cataloguing of the squadron's history is a monumental research effort. Unravelling some of the many mysteries of Babbage's record of service would have been considerably more difficult without the detective work of the Air Historical Branch's Seb Cox, but even he had to acknowledge defeat in some instances. I'm also grateful to my publisher, fellow cricket-lover John Davies, for his unfailing and good-humoured support; it makes working with Grub Street, and the company's fellow military authors, a genuine pleasure.

One such writer, Sean Feast, provided invaluable details on various Mosquito raids, not least in bringing to light the key role Ted Sismore played in the planning process. In the same way another author, the prolific and knowledgeable Chris Goss, offered extensive advice and assistance on all matters Luftwaffe. I'm grateful too to Natalie Parker, my editor, for her eagle-eyed assistance. Similar thanks go to David Ratcliffe, a wizard on the Merlin (pun intended) who went to considerable lengths to help me understand more about Spitfire engines.

I'm particularly grateful to Michael Rondot for permission to reproduce his beautiful Mosquito painting – and for the connection made through Antony Worsley's splendid Jet Art Gallery in Swansea. Dilip Sarkar provided extensive help on Battle of Britain details, likewise Andy Saunders. Both are masters of their subject, constantly revealing new truths and insights into the events of that summer of 1940. I'm especially thankful to the latter for his supply of supporting photographs and editorial advice – an unexpected bonus. Group Captain John Shields, Director Defence Studies (RAF), provided the key to unlocking early research problems, as did Ian Thirsk of the de Havilland Museum, who generously provided supporting photographs as well.

To each and every one of these individuals I reiterate my sincere and grateful thanks. While Cyril Babbage's story owes much to their important contributions, sadly there's still a great deal we'll never know about the life and times of one of those to whom Churchill rightly said we owed so much.

GLOSSARY

a/c	Aircraft
AE	Air Efficiency Award
AEF	Allied Expeditionary Force
AFC	Air Force Cross
AIB	Accidents Investigation Branch
AM	Albert Medal
AOC	Air Officer Commanding
AOC-in-C	Air Officer Commanding-in-Chief
ASR	Air-Sea Rescue
CAS	Chief of the Air Staff
CB	Companion of the Order of the Bath
CBE	Commander of the Order of the British Empire
CFS	Central Flying School
CH	Companion of Honour
C-in-C	Commander-in-Chief
CMG	Companion of the Order of Saint Michael and Saint George
CO	Commanding Officer
DFC	Distinguished Flying Cross
DFM	Distinguished Flying Medal

Do	Dornier
DSC	Distinguished Service Cross
DSO	Distinguished Service Order
E/A	Enemy Aircraft
EATS	Empire Air Training Scheme
F	Fighter
F/O	Flying Officer
FB	Fighter-Bomber
Fg Off	Flying Officer
Fi	Fieseler
FRS	Fellow of the Royal Society
FTS	Flying Training School
Fw	Focke-Wulf
GBE	Knight Commander of the Order of the British Empire
GC	George Cross
GCB	Knight Grand Cross Order of the Bath
GCMG	Knight Grand Cross of the Order of Saint Michael and Saint George
GCVO	Knight Grand Cross of the Royal Victorian Order
He	Heinkel
HE	High Explosive
HM	His Majesty
HQ	Headquarters
i/c	In charge
Ju	Junkers
KBE	Knight Commander of the Order of the British Empire
KCB	Knight Commander of the Order of the Bath
KCVO	Knight Commander of the Royal Victorian Order
KG	Knight Companion of the Order of the Garter
KT	Knight of the Thistle
MC	Military Cross
Me	Messerschmitt
Mk	Mark
MT	Motor Transport

MU	Maintenance Unit
NCO	Non-Commissioned Officer
NFT	Night Flying Test
OBE	Order of the British Empire
OC	Officer Commanding
OM	Member of the Order of Merit
ORB	Operations Record Book
OTU	Operational Training Unit
P/O	Pilot Officer
PC	Privy Councillor
Plt Off	Pilot Officer
POW	Prisoner of War
R&R	Rest and Recuperation
R/T	Radio Telephone
RAAF	Royal Australian Air Force
RAF	Royal Air Force
RAFVR	Royal Air Force Volunteer Reserve
RCAF	Royal Canadian Air Force
RFC	Royal Flying Corps
RN	Royal Navy
RNLI	Royal National Lifeboat Institution
RNZAF	Royal New Zealand Air Force
rpm	Revolutions Per Minute
RV	Rendezvous
SAS	Special Air Service
SFTS	Service Flying Training School
Sgt	Sergeant
TAF	Tactical Air Force
u/t	Under Training
USAAF	United States Army Air Force
USAF	United States Air Force
YMCA	Young Men's Christian Association

BIBLIOGRAPHY

BOOKS AND ARTICLES

Alcorn, John, 'Battle of Britain Top Guns – Update', *Aeroplane*, July 2020

Beevor, Antony, *D-Day: The Battle for Normandy*, Viking, 2009

Brew, Steve, *Blood, Sweat and Courage: 41 Squadron RAF 1939–1942*, Fonthill Media Ltd, 2014

Bungay, Stephen, *The Most Dangerous Enemy: A History of the Battle of Britain*, Aurum Press, 2000

Cossey, Bob, *Tigers: The Story of No. 74 Squadron RAF*, Arms & Armour Press, 1992

Feast, Sean, *Gestapo Hunter: The Remarkable Wartime Career of Mosquito Navigator and Leader Ted Sismore DSO DFC** AFC*, Grub Street, 2024

Fife, Malcolm, *A History of RAF Drem at War*, Fonthill Media Ltd, 2016

Golley, John, Gunston, Bill, ed., . . . *So Few – A Folio Dedicated to All Who Fought and Won the Battle of Britain*, WH Smith Ltd, 1992

Goss, Chris, *Jagdgeschwader 53 'Pik-As' Bf 109 Aces of 1940* (*Aircraft of the Aces, Vol. 132*), Osprey Publishing, 2017

Goss, Chris, *Knights of the Battle of Britain: Luftwaffe Aircrew Awarded the Knight's Cross in 1940*, Frontline Books, 2018

Hastings, Max, *Das Reich: The March of the 2nd SS Panzer Division through France, June 1944*, Zenith Press, 2013

Hastings, Max, *Overlord: D-Day and the Battle for Normandy 1944*, Michael Joseph, 1984

Herington, John, *Air Power Over Europe 1944–1945*, Australian War Memorial, 1963

Hillier, Mark, *RAF Westhampnett: During the Battle of Britain*, 80th Anniversary Booklet, self-published, 2020

Hodgson, Vere, *Few Eggs and No Oranges: a diary showing how unimportant people in London and Birmingham lived throughout the war years 1940–1945*, Persephone Books, 1999

Johnstone, Air Vice-Marshal Sandy, *Spitfire into War*, Grafton Books, 1988

Kingcome, Brian, *A Willingness to Die*, Tempus Publishing, 1999

McRoberts, Douglas, *Lions Rampant: The Story of No. 602 Spitfire Squadron*, William Kimber, 1985

Quill, Jeffrey, *Spitfire: A Test Pilot's Story*, Arrow Books Limited, 1985

Robertson, Air Marshal 'Black', *A Spitfire Named Connie*, Pen & Sword Books, 2022

Robertson, Air Marshal 'Black', *Fighters in the Blood*, Pen & Sword Books, 2020

Robertson, Air Marshal G.A. 'Black', *From Spitfires to Vampires and Beyond: A Kiwi Ace's RAF Journey*, Grub Street, 2023

Rowland, David, *Spitfires over Sussex: The Exploits of 602 Squadron*, Finsbury Publishing, 2000

Sarkar, Dilip, *Battle of Britain: Volume 1, The Gathering Storm – Prelude to the Spitfire Summer of 1940*, Air World, 2023

Sarkar, Dilip, *Battle of Britain: Volume 2, The Breaking Storm – 10 July–12 August 1940*, Air World, 2023

Saunders, Andy, *Bader's Last Fight: An In-depth Investigation of a Great WWII Mystery*, Grub Street, 2007

Shores, Christopher and Williams, Clive, *Aces High: A Tribute to the Most Notable Fighter Pilots of the British and Commonwealth Forces in WWII*, Grub Street, 1994

Shores, Christopher, *Those Other Eagles: A Tribute to the British, Commonwealth and Free European Fighter Pilots who claimed between two and four victories in aerial combat, 1939–1982*, Grub Street, 2004

Terraine, John, *The Right of the Line: The Royal Air Force in the European War 1939–1945*, Hodder and Stoughton, 1985

Vincent, David, *Mosquito Monograph – A History of Mosquitos in Australia and R.A.A.F. Operations*, David Vincent, 1982

Wellum, Geoffrey, *First Light*, Viking Press, 2002

PRIMARY SOURCES – THE NATIONAL ARCHIVES

AIR 27/425	41 Squadron ORBs
AIR 27/1924	464 Squadron (RAAF) ORBs
AIR 27/2075	602 Squadron ORBs
AIR 50/18/21	41 Squadron Combat Report
AIR 50/166/5	602 Squadron Combat Reports

ENDNOTES

INTRODUCTION

1 Later Group Captain Sir Douglas Bader CBE, DSO*, DFC*.
2 Later Air Vice-Marshal J.E. Johnson CB, CBE, DSO**, DFC*.
3 Later Wing Commander R.R. 'Bob' Stanford Tuck DSO, DFC**, AFC.
4 Major Erich Rudorffer, who retired with at least 219 victories to his credit.
5 A term broadly equivalent to the RAF's equally unofficial 'ace'.

CHAPTER 1

6 John Terraine, *The Right of the Line – the Royal Air Force in the European War 1939-1945*, p.43.
7 Ibid. p.44.

CHAPTER 2

8 The RAF was formed on 1 April 1918, merging the Royal Flying Corps with the Royal Naval Air Service.
9 Later Air Chief Marshal the Lord Dowding GCB, GCVO, CMG.
10 Then Air Chief Marshal Sir Cyril, later Marshal of the Royal Air Force the Lord Newall GCB, OM, GCMG, CBE, AM.
11 The timing of Gifford's combat report was 1445 hours while that of McKellar's was 1500.
12 Later Air Chief Marshal Sir Harry Broadhurst GCB, KBE, DSO*, DFC*, AFC.
13 The Supermarine Spitfire, designed by Reginald Mitchell CBE.
14 A pilot officer at the time, later Squadron Leader G.H.A. Wellum DFC.
15 Geoffrey Wellum, *First Light*, p.106.
16 Later Air Vice-Marshal A.D.R Johnstone CBE, DFC.
17 Later Group Captain A.D. Farquhar DFC.

18 L1007 was a prototype equipped with 20mm Hispano cannons prone to stoppages.

19 Later Air Vice-Marshal R.E. Saul CB, DFC.

20 As was the Commander-in-Chief Fighter Command, Air Chief Marshal Sir Hugh Dowding, and acting Air Marshal Richard Peirse, shortly to take over as Vice Chief of the Air Staff (his rank was confirmed in July), later Air Chief Marshal Sir Richard Peirse KCB, DSO, AFC.

21 This reference to McAdam as a flight sergeant is probably an error. Elsewhere in the ORB and in Johnstone's memoirs he is listed as a sergeant.

22 Such aircraft were used to deliver airmen and equipment in the early years of the war.

23 Squadron Leader A.A. McKellar DSO, DFC* was credited with 17 and three shared destroyed, five probables and three damaged enemy aircraft.

24 After repair it was transferred to 64 Squadron on 14 August 1940 as SH-W. Next day it was shot down near Calais. The pilot, Pilot Officer R. Roberts, was captured but the aircraft was subsequently recovered and test flown by the Luftwaffe.

25 Flight Lieutenant Donald Jack.

26 Malcolm Fife, *A History of RAF Drem at War*, pp. 36–7.

27 A powerful, portable beacon located at the end of a runway to assist pilots in landing, particularly in low visibility.

28 Squadron Leader R.J. Bushell was captured after crash landing and later masterminded 'the Great Escape'.

29 Johnstone was eventually credited with seven and two shared destroyed, one probable and six and one shared damaged.

CHAPTER 3

30 Dilip Sarkar, *Battle of Britain: Volume 2, The Breaking Storm, 10 July – 12 August 1940*, p.xv.

31 Later Air Chief Marshal Sir Keith Park GCB, KBE, MC*, DFC.

32 Squadrons of 12 aircraft generally flew in four sections of three: Red and Yellow for A Flight, Blue and Green for B Flight.

33 Air Vice-Marshal Sandy Johnstone, *Spitfire into War*, p.109.

34 Later Air Marshal Sir Richard Atcherley KBE, CB, AFC.

35 Awarded first annually and later biennially to the winner of a race for seaplanes and flying boats. After wins in 1927, 1929 and 1931, Britain retained the trophy permanently.

36 Later Group Captain J.R.A. Peel DSO, DFC.

37 Later Air Vice-Marshal J.A. Boret CBE, MC, AFC.

38 Except where transcribing from official documentation that refers to RAF West Hampnett, the one-word Westhampnett format is used throughout for Chichester/Goodwood.

39 Stephen Bungay, *The Most Dangerous Enemy,* p.200.

40 Ibid. p.218.

41 Discussed in more detail at Appendix 2, Babbage's claims.

42 Later Viscount Thurso KT, CMG, PC.

43 Bungay, *The Most Dangerous Enemy*, p. 231.

44 Later General the Lord Ismay KG, GCB, CH, DSO, PC.

45 While this damaged Me 109 is included in the summary at Appendix 2, it does not appear in other records of Babbage's claims, notably *Aces High*, Christopher Shores and Clive Williams.

46 Flying Officer W.H. Coverley was also known as Hugh.

47 David Rowland, *Spitfires Over Sussex*, p. 68, quotes Babbage's colleague, Pilot Officer Paddy Barthropp: 'A few brave buggers used to do head-on attacks. Bloody dangerous. There were one or two lunatics who revelled in it. The chance of hitting something going head-on was pretty remote unless you were attacking a big formation of bombers.'

48 Group Captain C.B.F. Kingcome DSO, DFC*.

49 John Golley, ... *So Few – A Folio Dedicated to All who Fought and Won the Battle of Britain*, p.163.

50 Ibid. p. 163.

51 At the time OC 74 Squadron, later Group Captain A.G. Malan DSO*, DFC*.

52 Luftwaffe records suggest that the returning raid Babbage attacked comprised He 111s of KG55; no Do 215s were lost on 26 August. While the two types were markedly different, it's possible that under fire Babbage misidentified his target. There's a related example of imperfect recall in his logbook, where his description of that afternoon's event is dated 27 rather than 26 August.

CHAPTER 4

53 1 Staffel (squadron/unit)/Jagdgeschwader (fighter wing) 53, known for its 'Pik As' (Ace of Spades) badge.

54 Officially the Knight's Cross of the Iron Cross.

55 Later Air Commodore J.E. Rankin DSO*, DFC*.

56 Air Marshal G.A. 'Black' Robertson, *From Spitfires to Vampires and Beyond: A Kiwi Ace's RAF Journey*, p.135.

57 Records of Mayer's claims differ: six to eight during the Spanish Civil War and 22–31 thereafter.

58 Flying Officer C.B. Willey, later awarded the MC.

59 Remarkably, X4187 was repaired and flying at 58 OTU, Grangemouth, just over a year later.

60 By Toovey's, Auctioneers and Valuers of Washington, West Sussex, with a reserve price of £30–50; it sold for £48.

CHAPTER 5

61 Johnstone, *Spitfire into War*, p. 166.

62 Bungay, *The Most Dangerous Enemy*, p. 309.

63 Later Squadron Leader O.P.V. Hanbury DSO, DFC*.

64 Later Flight Lieutenant E.W. Aries AFC, he eventually returned to flying as an instructor.

65 Rowland, *Spitfires over Sussex*, pp. 81–2.

66 Later Wing Commander P.P.C. Barthropp DFC*, AFC*.

67 According to a friend, New Zealander Wing Commander O.L. Hardy DFC*, AFC.

68 It would be lost two days later, when Sergeant Sprague was killed.

69 His final tally was two and two shared destroyed, one probable and three damaged.

70 Terraine, *The Right of the Line*, p. 208.
71 Johnstone, *Spitfires into War*, p. 178.
72 Ibid. p. 185.

CHAPTER 6

73 Bungay, *The Most Dangerous Enemy*, p.322.
74 Later the Lord Balfour MC*, PC.
75 Bungay, *The Most Dangerous Enemy*, p. 333.
76 Ibid. p. 332.
77 Ibid. p. 333.
78 Later Air Chief Marshal Sir Trafford Leigh-Mallory KCB, DSO*.
79 The aircraft designation appears in the ORB as 'Me 110 (? Jaguar)'.
80 Johnstone, *Spitfires into War*, pp. 188–9.
81 Daughter of the Marchioness of Anglesey, she later married Sir Richard Sykes.

CHAPTER 7

82 Terraine, *The Right of the Line*, p. 213.
83 Lady Diana Manners, a silent film actress and socialite who married Alfred Duff Cooper, Viscount Norwich.
84 Between half and full moon.
85 Vere Hodgson, *Few Eggs and No Oranges*, pp. 65–8.
86 Bungay, *The Most Dangerous Enemy*, p. 296.
87 John Alcorn, 'Battle of Britain Top Guns – Update', *Aeroplane*, July 2020, p. 27.
88 Bungay, *The Most Dangerous Enemy*, p. 293.
89 Ibid. p. 294.

CHAPTER 8

90 A group of popular entertainers formed in the 1930s comprising Bud Flanagan, Chesney Allen, Jimmy Nervo, Teddy Knox, Charlie Naughton and Jimmy Gold.
91 Later Marshal of the Royal Air Force the Lord Douglas GCB, MC, DFC.
92 Notwithstanding his later peerage, Dowding was treated shabbily and until his retirement in July 1942 effectively marked time in sinecures: a tour of the US on behalf of the Ministry of Aircraft Production then heading up a manpower study.
93 A small memorial to the 27-year-old Glaswegian, a metal plaque on a wooden shield, is fixed to a post near the spot where he died.
94 Later Group Captain R.F. Boyd DSO, DFC*, he was finally credited with 14 and two shared destroyed, three probables and two damaged.
95 Later Wing Commander A. McDowell, AFC, DFM*, he was finally credited with 11 and two shared aircraft destroyed in the air plus two probables.

CHAPTER 9

96 National Records of Scotland, https://www.nrscotland.gov.uk/.
97 These included *Mrs Miniver, Dangerous Moonlight* and *The Battle of Britain.*

98 Air Vice-Marshal J.O. Andrews CB, DSO, MC*, appointed AOC No. 13 Group on 4 February 1941.
99 Marshal of the Royal Air Force the Viscount Trenchard GCB, OM, GCVO, DSO.
100 Air Chief Marshal Sir Edgar Ludlow-Hewitt GCB, GBE, CMG, DSO, MC.
101 Later Wing Commander J.I. Kilmartin OBE, DFC.
102 Initials were used to differentiate between two Sergeant Browns; the other was W.M.
103 Later Air Commodore A.C. Deere DSO, OBE, DFC*.
104 Later Group Captain P.E. Meagher DSO, DFC.
105 MP for Bath at the time and later Group Captain T.L.E.B. Guinness OBE, he was one of the first private citizens to own an aircraft.
106 Sir Patrick Dollan, Lord Provost of Glasgow 1938–41.

CHAPTER 10

107 Later Group Captain D.O. Finlay DFC, AFC.
108 Squadron Leader H.R.L. Hood DFC; he is commemorated on the Runnymede Memorial.
109 Later Group Captain R.C.F. Lister DFC.
110 He was also captain of the British team for the 1948 Summer Olympics in London.
111 Keable was Rudorffer's 30th victim.
112 Coordinated bomber attacks on specific targets with fighter support.
113 Average of conflicting figures from *Blood, Sweat and Courage*, Steve Brew, p. 404, and A.M. Form 1180 related to p. 416 incident.
114 Brew, *Blood, Sweat and Courage*, p. 420.

CHAPTER 11

115 A few Mk II aircraft arrived on 602 Squadron towards the end of Babbage's tour.
116 Squadron Leader L.M. Gaunce DFC was hit by flak and killed when he ditched off the Cherbourg peninsula on 19 November 1941.
117 With a duodenal ulcer.
118 Shot down on the afternoon of 28 January 1942, he flew a sweep that morning with the author's father, then a sergeant on 72 Squadron (later Flight Lieutenant R.J.H. Robertson DFC).
119 Later Group Captain H.deC.A. Woodhouse DFC, AFC was posted missing in action, flying a Mosquito, on 13 August 1944.
120 Incendiary ammunition that produced flashes of light when it impacted a target.
121 Later Air Commodore Sir Archibald Winskill KCVO, CBE, DFC*, AE.
122 Also known as the Pat O'Leary line, organised by the French Resistance, it was one of the oldest and most important escape routes from occupied Europe for Allied soldiers and airmen.
123 Later Group Captain R.W. Oxspring DFC**, AFC.
124 Later Group Captain C.F. Gray DSO, DFC**, his final tally was 27 and two shared destroyed, six and four shared probables and 12 damaged.
125 Bungay, *The Most Dangerous Enemy*, p. 293.
126 Accidents Investigation Branch Precis Number W.1107A dated 27 February 1942.
127 Air Marshal 'Black' Robertson, *A Spitfire Named Connie*, p. 141.

128 A single-engined passenger/cargo aircraft, claimed incorrectly as a Ju 52.

129 A single-engined biplane trainer.

130 This was a misidentification. Although Sergeant Whiteford claimed a Ju 52 destroyed, it was in fact a Ju W34.

CHAPTER 12

131 Translates as Group Commander of 2nd Group, 26th Fighter Wing, named after Albert Leo Schlageter, a World War I veteran.

132 Chris Goss, *Knights of the Battle of Britain — Luftwaffe Aircrew Awarded the Knight's Cross in 1940*, p. 174.

133 Trejtnar bailed out safely, albeit with a shrapnel wound to his arm and a broken leg suffered on landing. His Spitfire crashed near the village of Black Dog, 15 miles north-east of Exeter.

134 Serving with the SAS, he parachuted into Italy, was captured and executed on 7 September 1943.

135 Jeffrey Quill OBE, AFC served on secondment with the RAF and Royal Navy Reserve during World War II.

136 Jeffrey Quill, *Spitfire: A Test Pilot's Story*, p. 206.

137 Ibid. p. 211.

138 Ibid. p. 210.

139 Ibid. p. 211.

140 Issued on 18 October 1942, it decreed that anyone captured while operating on commando raids against German troops, regardless of circumstances, was to be executed.

141 Quill, *Spitfire*, p. 211.

142 Captain John Verney, Special Boat Service.

143 John Huntington later described Pinckney as 'the best officer, man and gentleman, who I have ever met in my life'.

144 Later Group Captain R.J. Abrahams OBE.

145 Brew, *Blood, Sweat and Courage*, p. 515.

CHAPTER 13

146 Sebastian Cox OBE, Head of RAF Air Historical Branch, email 11 December 2024.

147 At the time Babbage had flown 17 different aircraft types; by the end of his career it was nearly 30.

CHAPTER 14

148 Terraine, *The Right of the Line*, p. 282.

149 He flew a Mustang 1 from Oatlands Hill, near Amesbury, on July 1942, transiting there and back from Upavon in a Harvard.

150 Formed 26 January 1943 and closed 6 April 1945, it handled conversions to the Oxford, Stirling and Halifax.

151 At the time Air Member for Research and Development on the Air Council, later Air Chief Marshal the Lord Freeman GCB, DSO, MC.

152 Later Captain Sir Geoffrey de Havilland OM, CBE, AFC.

153 L.C.L. Murray.

154 Group Captain P.C. Pickard DSO**, DFC was one of the RAF's most highly regarded bomber pilots.

155 Later Wing Commander R.W. Iredale DFC*.

156 They were fitted with delay fuses.

157 David Vincent, *Mosquito Monograph – A History of Mosquitos in Australia and R.A.A.F. Operations*, p. 75.

158 Flight Lieutenant J.A. Broadley DSO, DFC, DFM.

159 Later Marshal of the Royal Air Force the Lord Harris GCB, OBE, AFC.

160 Later Baron Zuckerman OM, KCB, FRS, at the time Scientific Director of the British Bombing Survey Unit.

161 Commander-in-Chief 21st Army Group, Allied Expeditionary Force, General Sir Bernard Montgomery, later Field Marshal Viscount Montgomery of Alamein KG, GCB, DSO, PC.

162 Terraine, *The Right of the Line*, p. 622.

163 General Dwight D. Eisenhower, later 34th President of the USA, 1953–61.

164 Franklin D. Roosevelt, 32nd President of the United States, 1933–45.

165 Terraine, *The Right of the Line*, p. 620.

166 Max Hastings, *Overlord – D-Day and the Battle for Normandy 1944*, p. 44.

167 Hastings, *Overlord*, p. 122 repeats the figure quoted in Terraine, *The Right of the Line*, p. 632.

168 Later Air Chief Marshal Sir Basil Embry GCB, KBE, DSO***, DFC, AFC.

169 Later Air Commodore E.B. Sismore DSO, DFC**, AFC, AE.

170 Air Marshal Sir Arthur Coningham KCB, KBE, DSO, MC, DFC, AFC, an Australian with the unlikely nickname of 'Mary'.

171 Published 10 October 1955, Volume LXVI Number 15.

172 The Oboe system coupled radar tracking with radio transponder technology, providing accurate positioning in any weather.

173 Hitler's 'terror weapon', a flying bomb nicknamed the 'doodlebug' – an early cruise missile.

174 Antony Beevor, *D-Day, the Battle for Normandy*, p. 49.

175 Ibid. p. 74.

176 Another example of the unique precision with which fatalities' details were recorded.

177 The SS (*Schutzstaffel*) was the elite guard of the Nazi regime, a virtual state within the Third Reich.

178 Later Major J.E. Tonkin MC.

179 McPhee's DFC citation referenced his 'high standard of leadership and outstanding devotion to duty'.

CHAPTER 15

180 Commander of the US 12th Army Group.

181 Known as *Leichte Eisenbahn-Transportschutz-Flakabteilungen* (Railway Transport Light Anti-Aircraft Protection Units) and under Luftwaffe command, 11 such flak units were raised in 1944 alone.

182 Vincent, *Mosquito Monograph*, p. 87, p. 118. From the transcript of a lecture Dunkley gave to the Aviation Society of Australia's New South Wales Branch.

CHAPTER 16

183 Panitz's navigator, Flight Lieutenant Williams, and Flying Officer L.C. Webb.

184 Later Wing Commander R.W. Reynolds DSO* DFC*.

185 Later Air Marshal Sir Peter Wykeham KCB, DSO*, OBE, DFC*, AFC.

186 Max Hastings, *Das Reich*, p. 207.

187 E.W.K. Walton GC, DSC. In 1948, as a temporary Lieutenant (E) RN he earned the Albert Medal (later the George Cross) for saving Tonkin's life in Antarctica when both were working for the British Antarctic Survey.

188 Kevin Walton and Gardon Robin, *Polar Record*, Volume 32, Issue 180, January 1996, p. 81.

189 The words of Generalfieldmarschall Gerd von Rundstedt, Vincent, *Mosquito Monograph*, p.87.

190 Later Wing Commander A.W. Langton DFC, AFC.

191 Why, and indeed how, anyone would record this meaningless figure is beyond the author's comprehension.

CHAPTER 17

192 The modern equivalent would be a Green Endorsement, the RAF's highest flight safety accolade: logbook recognition of exceptional skill and judgement in handling a potentially dangerous situation.

193 Later renamed as 9 FTS.

194 A village ten miles east of Taunton.

EPILOGUE

195 Christopher Shores and Clive Williams, *Aces High*, p. 11.

196 Golley, Gunston, . . . *So Few*, p. 163.

197 Sergeant (later Flight Lieutenant) P.L. Phillips, who retired in 1945.

198 Terraine, *The Right of the Line*, p. 45.

199 Golley, Gunston, . . . *So Few*, p. 163.

200 Ibid. p. 162.

201 Squadron leaders and above.

APPENDIX 1

202 Research suggests these aircraft were actually He 111s.

APPENDIX 2

203 At the time of the claim the aircraft was described as looking like a Curtiss Hawk.

INDEX

Where military ranks are shown, these are the highest reached by the individuals concerned.
n = endnote